Ivan the Terrible

Leaders From Ivan the Terrible to Stalin

(History of the Murderous, Bloodthirsty First Tsar of Russia)

Steve Pittman

Published By **Simon Dough**

Steve Pittman

*Ivan the Terrible: Leaders From Ivan the Terrible
to Stalin (History of the Murderous, Bloodthirsty
First Tsar of Russia)*

ISBN 978-0-9953115-8-9

No part of this guidebook shall be reproduced in any form without permission in writing from the publisher except in the case of brief quotations embodied in critical articles or reviews.

Legal & Disclaimer

The information contained in this book is not designed to replace or take the place of any form of medicine or professional medical advice. The information in this book has been provided for educational & entertainment purposes only.

The information contained in this book has been compiled from sources deemed reliable, and it is accurate to the best of the Author's knowledge; however, the Author cannot guarantee its accuracy and validity and cannot be held liable for any errors or omissions. Changes are periodically made to this book. You must consult your doctor or get professional medical advice before using any of the suggested remedies, techniques, or information in this book.

Table Of Contents

Chapter 1: Birth Of A Tyrant.................... 1

Chapter 2: A Menagerie Of Marriages ... 20

Chapter 3: Death Of A Princess; Murder Of A Nation.. 28

Chapter 4: Heirs To A Corrupted Throne 45

Chapter 5: The Sacking Of Novgorod, And Other Campaigns 66

Chapter 6: Heading For Defeat The Livonian War.. 83

Chapter 7: A Glimpse Of The Past Clears The Way To The Future.......................... 93

Chapter 8: Life Before The Tsardom: 1547-1560, The Early Years.......................... 104

Chapter 9: Ivan The Tsar Of All Russia From 1547-1560... 114

Chapter 10: All That Is Holy.................. 128

Chapter 11: The Wars And The Battles Lost And Won.. 141

Chapter 12: The Teror Of Ivan The Terrible: His Madness, Mania, And Murderous Methods 149

Chapter 13: Ivan's Final Years And Final Curse... 160

Chapter 14: Who Was Ivan The Terrible? 169

Chapter 15: His Youth 172

Chapter 16: His Domestic Policies And Rule 176

Chapter 1: Birth Of A Tyrant

It's getting' kind of heavy.

I've had been given the power! »

Ivan the Terrible

Ivan turned into born in 1530. His father become Vasily III, someone now not remiss himself at the same time as it came to carrying out what he needed to do to supply the energy he favored. After his father, Ivan III's, dying strength went to every one-of-a-kind son, the at the beginning named Ivan the Younger. But following this guy's fast loss of existence Vasily seized the throne, turning into Grand Duke of Moscow in 1505.

If our personalities are rooted in the genes we inherit, then there may be some excuse for the man Ivan the Terrible have become. Because his father too become possessed of vile moods and a vicious mood. This turned into not an uncommon trait among beyond

Russian Grand Dukes. Perhaps a lifestyles of absolute electricity, in which the slightest whim is met with unquestioning acquiescence, contributed to this. But if Russian Princes led by way of manner of way of worry many are recorded as possessing different, extra high nice, dispositions. Russia is a extensive united states of america; physical and climatically it is as severa as may be imagined. By the begin of the 16th century, it come to be one of the most powerful international locations in the international. That does now not appear with the useful resource of twist of fate. It comes approximately thru extremely good, organisation however forward-wondering manage. Sadly, this grow to be something Vasily did not own in abundance. He modified into in reality a bully.

And a childless one finally of maximum of his life. He married Solominiya Saburova, however the had been unable to conceive. With no inheritor at the horizon, and the possibility of the centuries-antique dynasty of which he come to be the fashionable, and in all likelihood very last, incarnation loss of lifestyles with him, he divorced the unlucky Solominiya and married Elena (on occasion written Yelena), the daughter of a fellow prince. They had two kids. Neither are served well with the useful resource of facts. The more youthful, Yury, come to be born deaf. It will not surprise many who any kind of physical or highbrow contamination turned into seen as unbecoming in a member of the aristocracy back in that day. However, Yury enjoyed the patronage of his excellent brother – an high-quality trouble genuinely, due to the truth that brother changed into none aside from Ivan the Terrible. Indeed, even as some interpretations of his lifestyles advise that Yury have become 'feeble-minded,' it seems no longer going that this become the case. For a brief time, on the identical time as his brother became away combating with the navy, he took entire control of country affairs. He additionally married and modified into a father to a son, albeit character who died in infancy.

Ivan have become really three years antique while his father died. Vasily superior a sore on his leg which in flip have become an abscess. The infection spread and painful lack of life end up endured. That dying threw Russia into turmoil. With the inheritor although a infant, others – the Boyar – fought for supremacy. Elena herself battled to be accepted as regent, but whilst Ivan changed into despite the fact that but a small boy, in reality eight years vintage, she too died. Elena changed into poisoned. It have become a way of loss of life that could come once more to keep-out Ivan lots later in his lifestyles.

THE BOYARS – RUSSIA'S CORRUPT ELITE

A quick diversion to visit the Boyars is now due. This is the term given to the numerous households of Russian nobility. They were an unimpressive lot. Like hyenas at some point of the bountiful gift that became Russia, they fought and schemed to seize the biggest share and sit down closest to the pinnacle. When that bountiful beast, in the form of Vasily, died, they flew proper into a frenzy of feeding, fighting tooth and nail to emerge as, so to talk, pinnacle hyena.

Not all the Boyars have been so willing; self-hobby did no longer occupy the waking mind of every member of this extended-established aristocracy but reliable, properly-this means that nobles had been few and a ways amongst.

Ivan might be Grand Prince, however his adolescence was wrought via terror. Both he and his brother were significantly mistreated with the aid of the Boyars. And while the home was a Kremlin palace, the time period 'jail' might possibly describe the situations wherein they existed more aptly. Armed men bestrode the corridors. As rival factions battled for supremacy, the boy in no way have end up extra than a tool to supply power to three formidable Boyar or special, and frequently an obstacle that stood inside the manner of them.

Fundamentally, the struggle for strength came all of the manner all the way down to an an increasing number of bloody warfare among outstanding families of Russian nobility - the Shuisky and the Belsky clans. Ivan and his extra younger brother have come to be pawns in this feud, alternately courted for their manual, then overwhelmed, robbed and abuse, however in no manner killed. It is hard to determine why.

But if the men survived, their closest confidents did no longer. The extra ruthless of the two factors, the Shuiskys, began out out to gain the top hand. Then, in 1539, they launched a raid at the palace and rounded up the majority of Ivan's ultimate loyal servants. The maximum relied on of those, Fyodor Mishurin, turned into skinned alive and left in a rectangular in Moscow to feature every a caution and a purpose for abuse by means of the usage of manner of the town's populace.

If children determines the individual, then Ivan the Terrible's dreadful exploits as an impregnable ruler can be traced once more to those early years. Parentless, unloved, with only a deaf more youthful brother as each pal and accomplice, Ivan threw himself into one situation he observed consistent – the scriptures.

The situations wherein Ivan lived bordered on the inhuman. He have emerge as now not often given food; he have turn out to be unnoticed. Sometimes he changed into abused. Physically, actually. Maybe worse. Remember, his father had not been a nicely-preferred chief so alongside the Boyar's war for manipulate of the usa of america the emotion of revenge bubbled threateningly in no manner a ways from the ground.

Indeed, given all of that, it's miles incredible that more younger Ivan changed into not, as was the case along together with his mother, eliminated from the photo. But although it in no way got here to pass, that fate emerge as one that grow to be constantly handiest a sword length away. Physically left out, emotionally humiliated, in my opinion insecure, from the age of 8 Ivan's adolescence have become a hellish as any is probably imagined.

A CHILD OF GOD

If the man or woman Ivan grow to be someone ridden with paranoia, it isn't always difficult to look from wherein that situation originated. But notwithstanding all of it, Ivan lived on. With no mother and father to shield him, he had to understand his protection as coming from someplace. The answer slowly emerged to the boy. He have become being blanketed by means of using God. The satisfactory safety that would ever be furnished. The seeds of megalomania have been planted, and they might be watered via his continued mistreatment on the hands of the ambitious Boyars.

The God of Ivan's revel in changed into the ferocious one of the Old Testament; one that received understand via worry, who ruled via retribution. The Old Testament is a bloody e-book; murders and massacres come to be regular happenings. Vehemence and violence are the norms. And that bloody chaos looms God.

From this biblical supply, the young Ivan located many commands. They have been not ones we might need upon a more younger, impressionable and scared toddler. Brutality and mercilessness, he got here to recall, have been the conditions of power. If he turn out to be to live to tell the story, then he needed to be robust. There was just one character of any significance in his lifestyles – that changed into his extra younger, deaf, brother Yury. If he too modified into to stay at the threats of the Boyars, then he ought to need an unflinching protector. Ivan decided to be that character.

A little historical mind-set helps us to recognize the strength of more youthful Ivan's religion. Today, the Russian Orthodox church even though exists but is a long way from a mainstream supply of religious steerage. But from the fifteenth Century, the opposite became the case. The Russian humans noticed their land due to the fact the middle of Christianity. Their church end up the right one, and consequently their chief emerge as the voice of God on the planet.

It is a effective conceit and one that can attraction strongly to a left out apprehensive young boy searching for a motive for his existence. Was God trying out him? Was he destined to be God's son in the world? It is straightforward to see how, locked away in his bloodless, harsh palace, such feelings can also need to emerge, then multiply.

Once more, we are able to hint the person he have end up again to the boy that he changed into.

Ivan's devotion have become obsessive. He might also bang his head time and again on the stone ground in advance than non secular icons. So plenty surely so he superior a callous on his brow. This excessive perception celebrated thru masochistic devotion would possibly live with him ultimately of his lifestyles.

Clearly, at the same time as a little one, Ivan changed into volatile. He must devote acts of sadistic cruelty on animals. Perhaps this obsession advanced from the satisfaction he gained from the self-inflicted struggling he persisted thru his immoderate devotion to God. Or in all likelihood he murdered animals simply due to the truth he loved doing it.

Nevertheless, Ivan ought to take small animals – puppies, cats, young bears – to the top of the tower of his palace and throw them via the open window areas to ruin at the ramparts below.

We apprehend from studies of sociopaths and psychotics these days that their character violence frequently grew from mistreatment of animals once they had been a infant. Ivan the Terrible ought to seem, on the face of it, a traditional case which illustrates this behavior pattern. The vicious, sadistic killer of fellows he should end up had its seeds within the violence he cherished committing on animals inside the direction of his formative years.

His torture of wildlife grew stronger. He might pluck the feathers from birds, then reduce their stomachs open. It turn out to be as even though each frustration in his small frame become exorcized thru his treatment of helpless creatures. It regarded as no matter the truth that maintaining their defenseless office work in his palms thrilled him in a way now not something else might also need to.

Over those small creatures, he was God. He decided whether or not or now not they lived or died. And, he decided on the method in their death.

A CHILD'S BID FOR POWER

But then, in 1539, the thirteen-yr-antique Ivan made his bypass. For all his savagery, he modified proper right into a studious, properly-have a look at boy and enough have turn out to be sufficient. It modified into time to behave in the direction of the Boyars. On December 29th he invited the Shuiskys to dinner and there launched a beautiful and savage verbal attack toward their chief, Prince Andrew Shuisky. Another corrupted and cruel Prince of Russia changed into approximately to meet his cease.

Ivan had him arrested and summarily thrown to a p.C. Of searching puppies. These were starved in schooling for this occasion and trapped in a constant enclosure. They fast found their prey. Ivan, the cruel but omitted boy, grew to come to be in a unmarried day into a leader in his non-public right. And now that cruelty which modified into a defining part of his individual need to flourish unchecked.

Many of the horrors Ivan ought to pass at once to inflict can be traced decrease returned to this time. Now it become human beings he focused, no longer animals. Even if helplessness remained a function of his sufferers. But no matter the strength the 13-12 months-vintage now loved, efficaciously unchallenged, he became despite the truth that a infant and a totally disturbed one at that.

Alcohol have become his drug of desire – probable it dampened down the terrors of his extra younger days. He obtained a gang of similarly elderly fans who started out out to terrorize the streets of Moscow. Soon, vandalism grew to become to assault. It end up now not lengthy before that crime escalated to rape. In foresight of the reign of terror to go back, there was no mercy proven to the patients he and his cohorts attacked.

Women and ladies were hung, thrown to bears and from time to time buried alive.

Soon Ivan determined a modern-day past time. He won a love of looking. It legitimized his endured delight of causing ache and suffering on animals. But quick the Grand Prince come to be satiated with the fun of looking boar and bears. He became his interest to a more realistic department of the animal worldwide, and farmers became his subsequent prey. He would possibly rob them and inflict upon them savage beatings. No doubt, many died at his arms. Indeed, on one event, he set his hounds on one in every of his servants, a member of his family who turned into no matter the reality that nice a boy.

The Russian human beings had been powerless to stop him. But via all this violence and cruelty, the more youthful Ivan endured in his devotions to God. They remained as severe as those prayers he completed as a younger toddler. If some thing, his exercise have become extra obsessional. He would possibly though throw himself in advance than icons and beat his head in competition to stone partitions, timber pillars, and floors. On one event, he even accomplished a public confession in Moscow. That have to have made an interesting, if genuinely debased, watch.

By his mid-young adults, Ivan turn out to be a complicated aggregate of extremes. Paranoid and savage embittered and vengeful, brutal but brutalized. If ever there has been a first rate instance of a younger psychopath, then the most effective guy within the then biggest us of a in the international ready that undesirable invoice. And just like the most disturbed people of any society, he changed into exhilarated with the aid of the energy he wielded, however additionally too rapid satisfied via way of way of it. Wider and wider sensory stimulation turned into required to fulfill his goals. This isn't unusual in psychopaths — it's far certainly that through using and huge those people aren't born into positions of perfect power.

RUSSIA'S DREAM — AT LAST, A TSAR

But for all his madness — it isn't possible to attract each different cease about this tyrant's intellectual us of a — Ivan become an smart more youthful man, properly take a look at and observed. As he approached his 17th birthday, he determined out that he needed to cement his feature at the pinnacle of the Russian pyramid of electricity. In January of 1547, Ivan introduced his impending coronation. Not, it need to be referred to, modified into the coronation introduced via a few zero.33 birthday party – it come to be an motion he decided upon himself. His father had been referred to as Grand Prince, a call he too had taken.

But that became no longer enough for a megalomaniacal psychopath. His God complex came to the fore, and he announced he would possibly turn out to be the Tsar of Russia.

This term comes from the Roman, efficiently enough in Ivan's case, for Caesar. The boy claimed direct descendancy from Rome, and as such he need to rule perfect over all homes of nobility. The role had now not previously existed, and it is as a substitute now not possibly that he became in any way descended from Roman aristocracy. But a name for for reality become not some issue held in specifically immoderate esteem with the useful resource of Ivan. Frankly, while you bear in mind that there has been no person organized to task the child's strength, he become capable of assume what he needed and act on his every whim.

For the Boyars, Ivan's idea become horrible news really (which also can, in issue, have been why he decided upon it). The call Tsar gave the holder sacred energy over them – their have an effect on can be right away faded. But as we've got seen, Ivan emerge as a clever, if wicked, leader. He understood that the Russian human beings have been unwell themselves of the corruption, the warring, the exploitation of the Boyars. They longed for a man they may name King. In Ivan, for all his manifold faults, that they had determined one.

Chapter 2: A Menagerie Of Marriages

«Sometimes I'm no longer certain what I hate more...honestly all and sundry or everything...»

Ivan the Terrible

At this detail, the more youthful guy's tale enters a realm that is a mixture among fairy story and gutter TV. He announced that he can also need to take a Russian bride – something similarly guaranteed to please his people – and would keep a country extensive virgin opposition to locate the female he would in all likelihood marry. It end up 1542 and Russia turn out to be entering into a period of fast exchange.

AN INFLUENCE FOR GOOD

Girls elderly twelve and above have been paraded inside the front of him; a few estimates located the figure at 1500. He made his desire – Anastasia Romanovna – no question after lengthy and cautious attention. Despite the extremely populist nature of the selection process to discover his bride, it became rarely a meritocratic manner. Anastasia have become herself the child of wealthy boyars, even though pretty second-tier individuals of the aristocratic Houses of Russia.

It also can moreover also be the case that the 2 had already met. Anastasia's uncle changed into one of the guardians who had guided Ivan most of the death of his dad and mom.

However, for some thing cause, Anastasia have turn out to be his decided on bride and astonishingly, given the doubtful nature of its origins, and the even extra dubious nature of the husband in the partnership, it changed into a marriage that flourished, marking the sanest and maximum managed duration of Ivan's life due to the truth the demise of his mother.

Indeed, the boy emerge as a calmer, greater tolerant (pretty speakme) guy as soon as his life have grow to be packed with proper love yet again. This gives some manual to the argument that his anger and volatility became located via his appalling childhood research, rather than inherited via some dubious own family gene.

Learned behavior may be controlled, inherited situations an awful lot a lot much less so. Anastasia and Ivan loved thirteen years of marriage. Despite its unsure origins, it does appear as even though there has been proper love many of the 2. Together, they had six children notwithstanding the truth that each one but died in infancy.

But it turned into Anastasia's person which seemed to bypass a benign impact on her unstable husband. She changed into able to snicker, and placed subjects into context, and this technique rubbed off on Ivan. The non secular man who spent plenty of his youth and early maturity bouncing amongst non-public flagellation for his sins and handing out torture and lack of existence to his citizens become calmed.

Even if Russia persisted to fight on many fronts for a fast period internal tensions have been eased.

A COUNTRY UNIFIED...AND DIVIDED

If subjects were better, they remained a long way from extremely good. In the yr following Ivan's coronation, Moscow fell sufferer to an inordinately excessive quantity of fires. Many have been killed inside the destruction, even as even extra were made homeless.

With no apparent target accountable, Ivan took the obligation for the fires onto himself. They have been, he determined, a punishment from God for his neglect about of his us of a. Ivan prostrated himself in a Moscow rectangular, swearing to protect his humans. It is part of the complexity of the man that, however the amazing horrors that he enacted on a subdued human beings, he took spiritual obligation for any failure – perceived or in any other case – that came his manner.

He may be in no way blamed for the fires that hit the town, but still, he took it upon himself to keep the burden for the destruction they delivered on – spiritually, if now not bodily.

Nevertheless, the fires delivered approximately reform. Ivan's manner of addressing the message God had despatched to him end up to alternate the order of society. He reformed the church and the military. He withdrew strength from the Boyars – a the Aristocracy already in detail castrated under his rule. In enacting these modifications, he modernized Russian society. It have come to be unified below him. Something that might had been to Russia's lengthy-term advantage had Ivan been a extra solid and empathetic man.

He modified into a man of God, one in the direction of God than a few other. Therefore, on account that God modified into excellent, so should he be. And that goodness needed to be loved via manner of others. Forcibly if critical.

THE TAKING OF KAZAN

He invaded and conquered the Muslim enclave of Kazan, which lay to the East of Moscow, keeping the achievement a spiritual victory. This emerge as an critical triumph, both for his popularity and strategic advantage.

Throughout present day statistics, normal invasions via the Tartars had happened. These incursions had been adverse to moral in addition to to the lives and wealth of the Russians they encountered.

Tartar manipulate of Kazan, a metropolis on the Volga, had prohibited use of that sturdy river as a route to the Caspian Sea, from which get right of entry to (and therefore change) can be discovered to special worldwide locations. In 1552, following careful arrangements, the Russian navy attacked the town and seized it. When, four years later, the very last Tartar stronghold at the Volga, Astrakhan, fell with out a combat, the Volga have become a Russian river, and the route to the Caspian Sea changed into secured.

He additionally understood that if Russia changed into to be the dominant international strain that God had determined it must be, then it needed to speak past its borders.

Opening the route to the Caspian Sea were an vital step on this path. Now Ivan opened trading links with the West, Britain. His marriage to Anastasia become turning in a golden age for the u . S ..

But golden some time have a addiction of completing all at once, with all the glory and pleasure of their times disappearing in a flash. Such an incidence passed off in 1560 at the same time as Ivan turn out to be thirty years old. One, deeply huge, occasion changed the us of the united states. Because it changed Ivan. For the extra excessive.

He preferred, steeply-priced and calming Anastasia died. And Ivan feared that her lack of life become the give up end end result of the foulest of play.

Chapter 3: Death Of A Princess; Murder Of A Nation

right right here became no apparent motive of Anastasia's loss of life. Although she modified into genuinely twenty-six years of age, and within the top of her existence, she fell sufferer to a protracted infection and one from which she have to in no way get higher.

But people do fall prey to ailment. Often ones unexplained via the fairly limited know-how of medicine man held within the 1500s. There had been many feasible causes that would have added approximately Anastasia's untimely lack of life. But to Ivan, there was no doubt about the cause of his loved's dying. She have been poisoned. And in addition, he had no qualms in deciding on the perpetrators of his accomplice's murder. It have turn out to be the Boyars, ultimately taking the maximum harsh form of revenge for his curtailment of their powers.

Despite his conclusions, he had no proof to all over again them up. Still, proof end up an non-obligatory costly whilst it got here to allotting justice under the Tsar's rule.

But earlier than we see how Anastasia's death did bring about the rightful addition of 'The Terrible' to her husband's name, we shift ahead in time for nearly five hundred years.

It has been handed within the legend that Anastasia emerge as poisoned, however handiest because of the fact the ones have been the words that Ivan ordered. However, researchers searching at life in the Kremlin's faraway bypass made a discovery which pointed genuinely to the fact that Ivan's deduction come to be correct. Most probable, that become because of paranoia infested risk in preference to accurate detective art work. Or perhaps a person did confess to understanding the truth about Anastasia's loss of existence. This character must well had been enduring the maximum agonizing of tortures on the time and feature come to be desperately welcoming the dearth of lifestyles which awaited round the corner. He may truely be encouraging it to go into the torture chamber and embody him. But none of this means that that that his confession lacked truthfulness.

However, modern technology has examined that the Tsaritsa changed into clearly poisoned, and the drug of choice which brought about her loss of lifestyles changed into that doyen of detective memories, mercury. When this metallic is ingested, the kidneys war hard to expel it, and the frame excretes as masses because the poison as it is able to through urine and sweat. However, its deadly outcomes however take keep, and death is a reality at the identical time because the poisoning continues. Some of the substance stays within the frame and continues to do its damage. The very last results is not often in question.

Scientists examined the frame of Anastasia preserved within the Kremlin and made the discovery that her hair retained massive quantities of mercury, most in all likelihood transmitted there thru sweat. Certainly, sixteenth-century makeup tended to include hundreds of lethal metallic and brought about the premature loss of life of many ladies. However, insufficient quantities can be absorbed through the pores and pores and pores and skin to supply the amount of the substance discovered in Anastasia's hair.

The identical scientists made a further discovery. Elena, Ivan's mother, had moreover been poisoned with the same killer chemical. That mercury changed into used in the deaths, almost 1 / 4 of a century apart, of the 2 closest girls Ivan ever knew or cherished, is too much of a twist of fate to dismiss.

While it typically seemed certain that the Boyars have been within the back of the death of Elena, committed in pursuit in their pursuits, now it appears the maximum powerful possibility that they had been also the killers of Anastasia.

Their motivations this time would possibly have been -fold. Firstly, for revenge in opposition to Ivan's past moves. Secondly, the demise of his preferred partner need to push the volatile Tsar again over the brink of sanity into the insanity that lay so near his floor. It changed proper right into a unstable method in the acute, but one that Ivan successfully, we now apprehend, detected.

The impact on Russia have become catastrophic. Without Anastasia, there was no longer any sort of mediating effect on Ivan. He might also want to conduct his regulations as he desired, with out a concept to the consequences they brought approximately.

While there was virtually resentment in the direction of him from some of the Boyars, normally the households of the nobility had been reliable. They fought in his armies and supported his regulations. That now counted for no longer something. Thirty years of anger grow to be bottled up internal of him, and the stopper became removed. With no calming accomplice, there has been no person able to staunch the go with the go with the flow of violence which poured forth.

The Boyars had been the primary victims. Children, girls, servants, princes, noblemen – no individual became spared from the torture. Boys as younger as twelve have been trouble to the same agonies that their fathers persisted till they in the long run surpassed some distance from their pain and indignity. A hurricane of terror changed into unleashed, and not anything provided secure haven from it.

A clean not unusual revel in infiltrated Ivan's thoughts. God had allowed his Anastasia to be taken. That turn out to be the act of a cruel and unthinking soul. If God acted on this manner, then the message he turned into sending to his apostle on the planet modified into the same. Ivan too want to rule cruelly, and irrationally.

SEEKING A NEW QUEEN – A SUCCESSION OF MARRIAGES

Whether in any manner it become a reputation that a spouse delivered a relaxing impact on him, Ivan attempted to duplicate the connection he had loved. He married no lots much less than seven instances following Anastasia's lack of life. Or possibly he married so frequently to satiate his lecherous sexual proclivity. Whichever is the greater sincere opportunity, that a immoderate range of marriages offers proof of the dissatisfaction the ones higher halves induced him. Or, probably, they inform us that now not anything may additionally want to stay as a bargain as his Anastasia.

The first lady to try to fill the shoes of his deceased loved become Maria Temryukovna. This courting lasted an less pricey quantity of time. Maria modified her name and transformed to Christianity to meet the Tsar's goals. She married him on twenty first September 1561, virtually months after her spiritual conversion.

Their marriage lasted for eight years, but she died in 1569. Rather like his first partner, the rumors have been that Maria become poisoned. But there the similarities amongst her and Anastasia stopped. Maria were round really 16 years of age (her date of beginning isn't always feasible to certify) even as she married Ivan. Already, even though, she have emerge as wild tempered and advise spirited. For Ivan, it have been her splendor that had been her enchantment. Anastasia had warned him to study out for Pagans – it seemed precise recommendation, due to the fact that, regardless of her conversion to Christianity,

Maria have become hated by means of manner of her subjects and, right away, with the beneficial resource of Ivan himself. He seemed her as too ungentrified to healthful into Moscow lifestyles, and her illiteracy positioned similarly distance some of the . Indeed, a few reminiscences put forward the concept that it modified into Ivan himself who poisoned her. If it come to be, his torture of numerous suspects following her lack of life might likely have proved to be an useless cowl for an act to which he may in no way must solution.

Together they bore a son, Vasyli, but he died as an little one. Probably, her vital contribution to his existence became that it end up she, in keeping with many resources, who endorsed Ivan to create his oprichniki, more about which we have a look at later.

Next to go back along come to be Marfa Sobakina...and she or he have turn out to be speedy to skip on. Ivan became however fond of choosing his better halves X-Factor style, and decided on Marfa from twelve 'finalists.' Unfortunately, her mother persuaded her to drink a potion that could boom her fertility, but as opposed to supporting her to conceive, it directly poisoned her. Within some days of her betrothal, she too turn out to be vain.

Perhaps her maximum considerable effect on Ivan's life changed into to make him even more paranoid than ordinary. Convinced that she were poisoned inside the secure partitions of his fort, he set approximately torturing and executing an entire lot of his court, alongside together with his former brother in law, Mikhail Temrjuk. Mikhail had been a huge and excessive best impact on his lifestyles, man or woman who had guided Ivan through a number of the best reforms he made. His suitable recommendation out of vicinity as a result of Ivan's uncontrollable mood might be something the tsar have to in no way update.

Never one to take a hint of any kind, and truly now not that marriage might not be for him. Ivan sought spouse amount four. The next unfortunate to earn his hand grow to be Anna Koltovskaya. This precise liaison almost did not materialize. That emerge as way to the Russian Orthodox church, which decreed a fourth marriage to be an impiety.

With the skills of a seasoned flesh presser, Ivan had been given round that specific hurdle via announcing that he had not consummated his zero.33 marriage. Presumably, he also can need to without a doubt as without trouble use his self-professed function as God's agent on this planet with the beneficial aid of really marrying anyway. It is not going each person may additionally want to growth too many objections. At least, no longer if they valued their lives.

However, this time he acquiesced to the Church's needs. The prelates required that he spend time with penitents; whether or not or for the way lengthy he adhered to that requirement we do now not realize. The glad couple honeymooned in Novgorod, which most effective two years earlier than he had ransacked. No doubt that made him a far much less than welcome visitor.

The marriage turn out to be doomed to failure. Anna Koltovskaya did now not conceive, and he dedicated her to a monastery. (A flow into he had enacted on higher halves of his son who did not endure human fruit.)

The manufacturing line endured. Next got here Anna Vasilchikova. Little is concept about Anna. Ivan determined to forego the church side of the wedding altogether this time. The had been now not married for extended. Again, she did now not proper away endure him a little one, so she determined herself swiftly dispatched to a monastery. Within a 12 months, this brand new of the Tsaritsas end up vain.

Vasilisa Melentyeva became the penultimate partner Ivan the Terrible decided directly to take. Or probably she changed into no longer. Some uncertainty surrounds Vasilisa. She might also additionally had been a widow once they married, or they'll no longer have ever formalized their liaison. That's the problem whilst little written facts remain of a tyrant's reign. There is lots of sitting at the fence.

The tale is that the Tsar determined this partner to be type and candy tempered. Perhaps, on this, she was most like his adorable Anastasia. However, he is also said to have positioned that she have become having an affair with a Russian prince. He proper away finished the amorous royal, making Vasilisa watch her lover's gradual and painful loss of life. She have become then solid proper proper into a palace cloister, in which she remained till dying.

But there are numerous inconsistencies surrounding Vasilisa. The lack of facts regarding her marriage to Ivan locations, in some historian's eye, Vasilisa's complete being into doubt. On the opposite hand, if she did marry the Tsar, it become with out the Church's blessing. Hence the shortage of written evidence in their liaison.

Lack of a wedding record does now not seem conclusive evidence of her non-existence. After all, the church had also did no longer bless his previous marriage, and variety four had only been granted after a warfare.

Other historians end that Vasilisa emerge as a concubine who surpassed in brief through the Tsar's existence. She might now not be the number one or final if that is the case.

But the evidence helping any marriage she had with the Tsar is likewise flimsy. There are fine two mentions of her in Russian statistics books. The first virtually lists her in passing as a prostitute. The principal file of her lifestyles have come to be written with the useful resource of Alexander Sulakadzev. Unfortunately, he isn't always a reliable supply; his writings -made inside the early 1800s - having been uncovered as fraudulent.

Whether she existed or not, there can be neither dependable file of her time as Ivan's partner, neither is there a grave or memorial to her, as a minimum no longer one that has but been placed and identified.

Last and truely possibly least of the Tsar's legitimate betrothals was to Maria Nagaya. Once extra, the Orthodox Church was excluded from the method, Ivan with the resource of now feeling he had a proper away line to God. To be honest to terrible Maria, while she have become something however one in all Ivan's favorites, by the time they married in 1581 his fitness became fading, he end up maximum probably stricken by rheumatoid arthritis and really probable a bunch of different situations. To say he emerge as not often the most affable of humans is a real understatement of large proportions but with the aid of the usage of this element in his lifestyles, he changed into at his most ferociously volatile.

That Maria remained his partner until his lack of life is a testomony to her staying powers...and the fact that she did go through him a son. To offer an idea of the low regard in which she come to be held by using the use of manner of the tsar, he contacted Queen Elizabeth in London, presenting to desert Maria to marry the Queen's cousin. The type offer was rejected. By this issue, Ivan the younger became useless, and Ivan IV had little faith in his extra youthful son, Feodor. So, the advent of Dmitry in 1582 was a welcome remedy, and probably saved Maria the future that had befallen a number of her predecessors – being robust out to a monastery.

However, as a signal of the dismissive way he held in the path of her, Ivan left not anything to Maria in his will, and he or she emerge as compelled to stay off the income of her little one son. He have been granted Uglich, a border town at the River Volga. Sadly, more youthful Dmitry died from a seizure at the identical time as nonetheless a small boy.

Chapter 4: Heirs To A Corrupted Throne

proper here have been different big human beings in Ivan's life. His sons, Ivan and Feodor. Ivan have come to be the fave. Like his father, he changed into properly observe and savage. He enjoyed not whatever more than to look at the oprichniki at their paintings. Once, a prisoner through the choice of Bykovski seized a sword and raised it to attack Ivan senior. His son stepped in and stabbed the have to-be assassin. It is deeply ironic, therefore, that the younger Ivan may also sooner or later die at his father's fingers.

Ivan changed into set for marriage on the age of twelve to the daughter of the King of Sweden, Virginia Eriksdotter. That got here to not some thing, but he did wed on the age of seventeen...to one of the ladies his father had rejected on the equal time as selecting his spouse following Anastasia's loss of life. The concept grow to be to provide an inheritor, but even as that did no longer arise the terrible woman, Eudoxia emerge as banished to a convent. She became quickly joined, for the equal purpose, with the resource of the usage of Ivan's 2nd spouse, Praskovia Solova. Only with the useful resource of manner of the 1/3 try, to Yelena Sheremeteva, should an inheritor be conceived.

If Ivan grow to be the favourite who shared many of his father's tendencies, then his extra youthful brother Feodor really did no longer. Weak-willed, possibly intellectually disabled he bore not one of the ambition of his father and brother. History information him as kind and slight. He did keep the Rurik dynasty, which had dominated for hundreds of years, after his father's lack of existence and did turn out to be Russia's 2nd tsar.

But Ivan the Terrible's actual dynasty became unique to him – best his eldest son ought to have carried that ahead. Indeed, no matter ruling in name, while Feodor in the end ascended to the throne, in exercise the united states of a have emerge as led through his brother-in-law.

Feodor died childless, and Russia – already crumbling – fell into trendy disarray.

IV A TYRANT'S AGONY

"I will no longer see the destruction of the christian converts who are reliable to me, and to my final breath I will combat for the orthodox faith."

Ivan the Terrible

However, there is but every other element which contributed in a few techniques to the floods of violence Ivan IV undammed upon his human beings. That problem emerge as his deteriorating physical health. We can be as high-quality as statistics allows that Ivan the Terrible emerge as mentally unhinged. Most in all likelihood, that have turn out to be in big part a cease result of dropping his mom at an early age, of in no manner records his father and, on pinnacle of all of it, experiencing a teenagers of terror and fear, abused and omitted in same portions.

Given his father's erratic conduct, and the recognition of many for the Grand Princes who predated him, it is a now not unreasonably jump of religion to complete that his instability also can moreover had been genetic.

ILLNESS OF THE BODY

But we noticed that under the have an impact on of his masses loved first partner he might also moreover want to control the excesses of his conduct. During that factor, he pulled Russia together. The stress of his will overcame dissent and distrust. He have to act for correctly.

As he got older, some different have an effect on modified into playing a merciless element in his very personal story, and that of his country. Two closely loosely related influences which added approximately a

3rd, ironic scenario which certainly brought to his psychosis.

Ivan the Terrible suffered from rheumatoid arthritis. Examinations of his stays done in the Nineteen Sixties provided undeniable evidence of this. Rheumatoid arthritis is a debilitating situation. Even with present day arsenal of drug treatments and ache killers, it remains an agonizing infection. Imagine the endless ache reverberating via his frame. His suffering may be worsened via the bloodless conditions of the lengthy Russian winters. Such a country could only grate away at a damaged thoughts. Nobody, it'd seem to him, have to expose greater devotion to his God. That identical God continued to punish him. It changed right into a conundrum to which he couldn't come to phrases.

It seems specifically probably that Ivan additionally suffered from syphilis. The disease changed into rampant in sixteenth-century Russia, as really it changed into in the course of masses of the world. Sexually transmitted, maximum promiscuous had been the most prone to its undesirable and painful tentacles. Few have been extra promiscuous than Ivan the Terrible.

We understand from his days as a teens that Ivan have grow to be pushed by way of sexual goals. Those yearnings decrease lower back and flourished in his located up-Anastasia adulthood.

Affairs, casual sex, rape, enslavement. All were regular pages in his life's tale. And Ivan changed into no longer overly particular nearly about who it come to be unwillingly pressured into his bedchamber. Men, boys, ladies, girls...his tastes had been eclectic in the acute. In such events, it is hard to see how his body couldn't be riddled with sexually transmitted infections.

Symptoms of syphilis include tiredness, headaches, flu-like pains and ache in the joints. The disease can live latent in someone, reappearing at normal durations.

So, we discover our violent, heartless and cruel chief with moods worsened thru a combination of regular ache and a enjoy that God will no longer forgive him for some thing sins the Great Being has decided he has devoted. As we observed earlier, capsules of 1540 were simple and typically prone to motive more damage than top. With a painful irony, Ivan could not have recognized at the time, one of the most commonplace varieties of remedy have emerge as moreover one of the most volatile. For joint contamination, an average treatment changed into to prescribe mercury. The very poison that nearly certainly killed his spouse and mom changed into one he took himself in a failed try to relieve the normal ache from which he suffered.

We recognise, from the research of his remains, that his body contained enormous quantities of mercury. Of course, this can be evidence of an try and poison him within the same way his accomplice and mom were dispatched, despite the fact that this is a miles a whole lot much less probable possibility than an try and alleviate his symptoms and signs and symptoms.

ILLNESS OF THE MIND

But mercury does more than truly poison the body. It alters the thoughts. Its impact on the thoughts can be catastrophic. It leads to violent temper swings and outbursts of irrational, uncontrollable temper. Here is a paranoid psychotic bearing the added burden of a poisoned thoughts. Such a mixture offers some belief into the reasons for the savagery of his reign of terror.

As we attempt to research the causes for the kingdom of his mind, we see how complex this changed into. His intense violence closer to animals as a infant is a not unusual forerunner to immoderate violence in maturity. The raping, torturing and murdering that located after he seized control as a thirteen-year-vintage is similarly proof of a deeply disturbed thoughts. And all over again then he couldn't call on the protection of being poisoned via way of mercury. The length of relative calm which rippled outwards sooner or later of his marriage to Anastasia proved that he may need to, underneath high-quality conditions, moderate his conduct.

But as an older man, his excessive violence can be discovered through bouts of excessive melancholy as he observed the effects of his uncontrollable mood. These aren't the developments we want to peer in a leader. Particularly no longer whilst that leader is blessed with absolute, unquestioned, energy. That authority can be seen in physical form within the lengthy, ornate and lethal employees he always carried. A lethal weapon topped with a golden detail capable of wounding...or killing. The photo of this despot is complete. It isn't a pleasing one.

THE GREATEST GAMBLE

In 1565 the Tsar made the strangest of selections. He added that he could abdicate, that the hassle and unrest inside the u . S . Changed into now not the give up result of his megalomaniac behavior, however the surrender give up result of sedition thru the evil Boyars who sought to blight him (and his human beings) at every turn.

The statement changed into almost really made for political gain. Although it modified right into a spur of the immediate selection made in anger can not be disregarded. Most cutting-edge historians agree with that his assertion have become to gain leverage along together with his humans. He gambled on the perception that the townsfolk, the peasants or perhaps the Boyar themselves could not ponder a rustic with out the figurehead of a tsar, as scary as having one is probably. As an lousy lot as all feared him, so he grow to be seen as vital through his humans. Society is a extraordinary beast. As the population noticed it, the selection going via them lay among tyranny and utter chaos.

That former opportunity have end up, with the aid of maximum, visible as the slightly higher desire of two horrible options.

Many ought to keep in mind the corruption and catastrophes of the leaderless times on the same time as Ivan turn out to be even though a infant. As awful because the possibility turn out to be proving to be, a go back to that chaos could likely virtually be worse. So, the people selected to collect in the again of the tsar. His ploy had paid off. Senior participants of the the Aristocracy, together with crucial individuals of the clergy held a thriller meeting, and from that elected to beg the tsar to preserve as their chief.

Ivan agreed, but he had a rate. The price of his persevered management became immoderate. He favored the right to a unfastened hand to purge his u . S . A . Of a few issue he noticed in shape and to gain this with out worry of competition or complaint. There are masses who may also want to argue that this have become, anyways, what he was doing. But now he have to carry out his purges officially, with a license to perform that signed thru greater than absolutely himself.

And that meant, to his twisted mind, that he changed into now the best interpreter of the will of God. Effectively, he become God among his humans.

But even a God goals someone to carry out his grimy artwork. Ivan's first step grow to be to create his secret police, a private bodyguard to adopt his each need. He successfully reduce the u . S . A . Into . Russia is a significant mass of varied land. From ice blanketed barren place, via to wealthy and fertile plains; from regions with insufferable versions in climate to others whose climate is the identical of any within the international. It is not any surprise that those more temperate areas held the wealth of the u . S ., whilst the alternative, bleaker outposts had been populated through peasants.

Ivan had little interest inside the ones poorer components. To control them right away might also region an large burden on his property. So, as a on hand sop to the Boyars, he left them to run the maximum barren, most impoverished factors of the brilliant u . S . A .. Even then, those who survived paid a similarly price.

A latest archaeological discovery shed moderate onto one of the responsibilities of the Boyars who had been legal to live as part of the Russian the Aristocracy. The discover modified into a massive arsenal. The weapons contained inner covered bows, sabers and spears. Articles of uniform additionally survived, which includes the leather-based-based totally belts worn by using the tsar's mystery military and the pointed hats that adorned their heads.

The find out became in an vintage timber cellar, the house above it having burned down centuries earlier than. The weapons had been perfectly preserved and unused. The implication modified into that the Boyars might be required to host squadrons of Ivan's model of the Gestapo, feeding and sheltering them as a standing unit who have to head to conflict if referred to as upon. Ivan the Terrible's army machine in reality became complex and powerful.

THE OPRICHNIKI – THE TSAR'S SECRET POLICE

Meanwhile he, via this mystery military called the oprichniki, straight away ruled the richest regions. It became a rule marked by means of using ruthless cruelty.

In many methods, Ivan the Terrible's regime echoed Russia of the Soviet Union some 4 hundred years later. The thriller police of the communist regime of Stalin – the KGB – may be represented by using his navy of oprichniki.

This police had been fearsome. Dressed all in black, they rode black horses that have been decked out in the severed heads of puppies.

With a touch that might be humorous had those men now not been so savage they carried brooms as symbols of their reason to comb away any wrongs. Faults which, of course, have been perceived as such with the beneficial resource in their chief. This frightening series of fellows consisted of the maximum terrifying in Russia. Many have been criminals of the most ruthless, heartless variety. Most have been hand-picked with the useful resource of Ivan, who sought out the most harsh guys he need to discover.

We used the time period 'police' in advance, but in reality, this modified right into a misnomer. These had been not up keepers of law and order. Not even criminal suggestions generating from a central authority which used fear as its agent of manipulate. They were legitimized criminals. Simply, they swept thru the Russian geographical location and cities, raping, stealing, killing. They took some thing they preferred. And did so with the authority of Ivan behind them.

But even in an employer as corrupted because the oprichniki a hierarchy exists. Ivan took the three hundred individuals of his secret police who he identified as the most vicious, maximum cut-throat and established them as his guard in his palace. A palace which, with unknowing irony, he referred to as his 'monastery.'

It become an top notch region. In some techniques, its practices did mirror those of a immoderate church monastery. Ivan was nevertheless besotted through his devotion to God. It changed into just that his grow to be a God that none should recognize; a threatening, evil creature who stable out plague and struggling on His humans. And if it modified into proper enough for God…then that turn out to be accurate enough for Ivan.

Like some extremely-non secular monastic residence, lifestyles on the palace ran to a respectable time desk – one that have become immeasurably harsh. Ivan himself have to start the day at 3.00 am, ringing bells to summon his defend to the church for prayers. And each of those guards had higher be prepared to upward push inside the icy darkish. Failure to attend prayers brought about prison – no longer an area in which any may want to want to spend time.

The issuer that observed become little more than a general performance to a captive audience. Ivan would sing, chant, beat himself and prostrate himself earlier than his altar. This need to preserve for four hours. Sleep would possibly comply with, at the facet of a quick meal. Then, while the morning moved to the afternoon, the amusing may additionally start.

Ivan used this part of the day to visit his dungeons. Most frightening of all amongst these modified into Ivan's torture chamber. Within its walls he created hell. Punishment there has been of biblical proportions. Those unlucky sufficient to have encountered his wrath sufficiently to discover themselves on this room may additionally need to sit up for no longer whatever but no longer possible suffering.

Sometimes Ivan can be a pleased observer to the torture that took place every afternoon; an excited member of the aim marketplace to the general overall performance provided to entertain him. A show, of route, whose predominant man (or female, or little one) could as an alternative be everywhere else. At one-of-a-kind times,

Ivan took an active characteristic in court docket docket cases, casting himself as a torturer in leader. A witness from the time described how Ivan would leave the torture chamber smiling in contentment.

Perhaps, given an exceedingly tolerant element of view, the immoderate spiritual observance of the mornings is probably excused as an overzealous devotion to God. Even the afternoon's torture training can be considered as a out of location try to cleanse the region of evil. But the very last part of an regular day at Ivan's palace come to be truly not possible to justify in even the broadest, maximum tolerant view of what constituted everyday the spiritual exercise because of the fact the very last greater of the day became a sexual one. An orgy, imparting unwilling peasants, ladies, boys, women, compelled to have interaction in the most bizarre of practices with Ivan and decided on contributors of his mystery police. Raped, whipped, sodomized — even used as stay purpose exercise these younger unfortunates had been pushed into hell. Often, they might never go away. At least, not at the same time as no matter the reality that alive.

Death have become moreover an undesirable final outcomes going via landowners and Boyars who fell victim to the rampaging oprichniki. Conservative estimates located the sort of sufferers killed via the ones warriors as ten thousand – many more have been forcibly evicted from their land and homes, that have been, in turn, taken over through the usage of Ivan's marauding forces.

Nobody have to project Ivan's wanton supremacy. On one event the pinnacle of the orthodox church pleaded for mercy to be established closer to some men accused of rebelliousness. Not handiest did his pleas fall on deaf ears, however he too have grow to be arrested, charged with sorcery, tortured and killed. Russia below Ivan changed into not an area to elevate one's head above any parapet, but low that protective wall is probably.

Chapter 5: The Sacking Of Novgorod, And Other Campaigns

«To shave the beard is a sin that the blood of all the martyrs can't cleanse. It is to deface the picture of man created by way of the usage of God.»

Ivan the Terrible

It become now not even important to provide any opposition, but minor, to draw the attention of the tyrannical Tsar. The records that the metropolis of Novgorod have become planning to rebellion became in no manner greater than an unsubstantiated rumor. Ivan desired no more. He already had his vindictive and paranoid eyes at the unproblematic settlement. A twelve months before his ransacking of the metropolis he had evicted severa residents from every Novgorod and the adjacent city of Pskov at the off chance that there is probably sedition inside their town partitions.

A couple of years in advance than he had misplaced, then regained, the town of Izborsk, and grow to be terrified that this become a sign of growing and large treason. His fears were primarily based on no longer anything however out of vicinity intuition and neurosis.

Then, within the months principal as a good deal because the sacking, he finished Prince Vladimir and masses of his own family, He drowned Vladimir's mother and spouse. It is likely greater than a passing coincidence that numerous Vladimir's surviving friends lived in Novgorod. The execution of the Prince became normal of Ivan's conduct at some point of the latter part of the 1560s. Recovering from contamination, he approached the Prince – who occurred to moreover be his cousin and gave him the honor of turning into his very own son's regent within the occasion of his loss of existence.

But something changed his attitudes within the course of Vladimir, and in 1569 the executions befell. No similarly explanation modified into coming close to. Except, possibly, that Ivan changed into definitely mad.

AN UNNECESSARY REVENGE - NOVGOROD

In 1570 he ordered his oprichnik to attack the metropolis. The attack does now not do justice to the ferocity of their advertising and marketing campaign of terror. For 5 weeks, the name of the game police sacked the metropolis, massacring, capturing, torturing, raping the populace. Nobody became secure. From the youngest peasant infant to the matriarch of a community Boyar. All have been assignment to random, unjustifiable cruelty. The attack has entered, for all the wrong reasons, into the folklore of Russian lifestyle. It became immortalized in Tchaikovsky's opera, 'The Oprichnik,' and Vasnetsov's portray, 'The Street inside the Town.'

If there was to be a justification for his attack, and Ivan did like in order to supply an reason for away the excesses of his conduct, it emerge as that the city's Boyars had been planning handy it over to the growing Polish and Lithuanian Commonwealth, itself a sworn enemy of Ivan. Their seditious act changed into to be aided through Bishop Pimen, the archbishop of the city.

However, it appears that naturally there has been little proof to manual this idea, no matter the fact that some historians accept as true with that retailers of the commonwealth can also have planted papers to destabilize the tsar (a circumstance which, it's far steady to mention, modified into already properly underway.)

On sixth January, Ivan arrived outdoor the town with fifteen-twelve months-antique Ivan and some 1500 troops. He ordered that senior clergy member and monks be rounded up, and people have been finished on tomorrow, overwhelmed to dying in advance than being another time to their monasteries for burial.

On the 8th, Ivan the Terrible advanced to the Volkhov river, wherein he grow to be met with the resource of the Archbishop. This have grow to be a traditional courtesy extended to senior individuals of society and, despite the fact that the subsequent conference, an strive become made thru using Pimen to bless his tsar. The gesture became rebuffed, and as an alternative Ivan made his accusation of treachery in opposition to the churchman, and in turn, the town.

But we see the disturbed kingdom of Ivan's thoughts via what occurred next. He demanded to be taken to the cathedral in order that he should take divine liturgy. Later, he insisted on being hosted via way of manner of the Bishop. Each of the above came about in the chaos of a pillaging raid. Pimen end up arrested as their meal started out out, his residency became plundered, and the Archbishop publicly humiliated.

For some thing he need to try and justify as a non secular and political cleaning, Ivan's moves regarded to be more tied to economic benefit than might be predicted. Churches, cathedrals and monasteries have been stripped of their treasures.

Operating on the precept that high-quality fortunes are built on pennies, he even ordered town clergy to be flogged until they handed over the sum of twenty rubles.

While the improvised courtroom at the tsar's make do Gorodische camp became starting to wind down – there are simplest such quite a few officials to attempt to execute – the ransacking of wealth from the metropolis persisted unabated, with Ivan himself frequently overseeing the art work of his oprichniki. What couldn't effects be stolen away turned into demolished; church bells were forged to the ground, farm animals were slaughtered, church elders were punished virtually due to the reality they will be.

But as awful because the stripping of the metropolis's property is probably, it have grow to be the remedy he done inside the course of the city's populace that most horrifies, though so extra than four centuries on. Some of this wickedness was directed in opposition to unique people of the Boyars and the middle schooling. At different instances, there occurred virtually a acquainted slaughter of the peasantry.

False confessions have been given below torture, implicating particular harmless humans in the treason Ivan claimed to suspect. Torture included being grilled over a giant frying pan type device; others were hung by way of the use of their palms, and their eyebrows singed away.

Young children had been thrown into the freezing Volkhov river. There patrolling oprichniki prepared with spears and lances driven any that controlled to surface lower decrease back beneath the cracked ice.

When the pains had completed, propelling numerous hundred nobles, statesmen and clergymen to a painful and untimely loss of existence, the oprichniki opted for a quicker direction to growing the tsar's coffers while concurrently crushing any lingering perception of revolt.

Houses had been pillaged and destroyed, on the side of any inhabitant who may item. Often, whilst the temper took him, an oprichniki would honestly kill a house owner, or their kids, for the easy pride of doing so. These picks may be justified as urgent home the lesson of the futility of opposing the tsar (no longer that, in any case, these human beings have been thinking about such an movement). At wonderful instances, residents were randomly dragged in advance than Ivan simply so he need to exercise his sadistic styles of torture, alongside together with his son searching at the sidelines.

In all, it is belief that 15000 people died as a proper away end result of the sacking of Novgorod. Countless more perished because of the reality their homes had been destroyed, and they have been forced out into the unforgiving Russian wintry weather, without a refuge to shield them from the snow, ice and sour winds. Figures for the overall amount of deaths which resulted from the attack range from ten thousand to 60000 all counseled. The lower tremendous range is based totally totally on the fact that the town had presently suffered famine and outbreaks of sickness, so the population grow to be low besides. The better parent makes use of the standard amount of the town's population.

It is unhappy that, while each death represents the suffering of a person and the snuffing out of life, information are so indistinct.

As come to be his wont, Ivan misplaced interest a few days into the slaughter, taking an an increasing number of lower again seat, however the oprichniki persevered their suppression until mid-February in advance than transferring right away to comparable invasions of various towns. The tsar's rule become likely the most sadistic in the mentioned information of mankind, and the destruction of Novgorod its maximum immoderate deed.

If the horror of Novgorod teaches us some detail we did not already recognize approximately this barbarous tyrant, it is an notion into his want to justify his moves. There can truely be no doubt that, at the same time as the slaughter modified into going on, he have become pleased with the aid of the torture, ache, and struggling he inflicted on his often harmless sufferers. But it emerge as similarly vital to Ivan that he may be justified in his cruel moves.

He wished confessions. He needed to understand that his moves have been a turning into punishment for one which strayed. And he could inflict some thing ache have turn out to be essential to draw those confessions. It is a bizarre scenario; a man inflicting the most no longer possible levels of ache to someone to draw the terms that vindicate the infliction of that suffering.

We see in Ivan the paranoia, the psychotic behavior of the sociopath. He enjoys causing suffering however must additionally rationalize his conduct in doing this. He want to receive as real with that his moves are proper and right inside the eyes of God. It is delusional behavior, enacted by using using character who is privy to no boundaries, and on whom no limitations may be imposed.

ON TO MOSCOW

Novgorod become not by myself in feeling the ire of a frontrunner out of manage. Moscow suffered too, as did the metropolis of Pskov. Fearing competition to his movements in Novgorod, he focused the slight noblemen of the metropolis. A mass trial followed.

Its final outcomes end up in no way unsure. Under his nowadays constructed cathedral in Red Square, eighteen scaffolds were erected. Near them, alarmingly, turn out to be placed a huge cauldron. It changed into filled with water, and underneath it, a big hearth come to be lit.

Once more, Ivan wanted his target audience. Moscovites had fled on the website of the arrangements, but now they have been rounded up and dragged to the square to witness the bloodbath about to seem. Hundreds have been completed on the first day of the witch hunt by myself. Members of the navy, of america of a, of the Boyars – all can be dreams. Playing to his crowd, Ivan showed he may be benevolent in addition to fearsome. He approached the terrified captives and prolonged his benign forgiveness, pardoning round one hundred and 80 of the terrified prisoners.

According to records, the primary to die emerge as a statesman referred to as Viskoyati. Ivan struck him powerfully at the pinnacle as he have a look at out every trumped-up fee. Viskoyati screamed his loyalty and innocence, but it modified into to no accord. He have become strung the opposite manner up and his ear lessen off. Then slowly, painfully his frame have become hacked to quantities, a limb at a time until he must scream no greater. The 2nd victim to be hauled ahead modified into a friend of Viskoyati; the metropolis treasurer, Funikov-Kartsev.

He changed into subjected to the equal remedy as his now deceased pal. And so, it persevered, the group baying its assist, stuck up in a mixture of blood lust mixed with fear for doing some element however provide easy and vocal help for their Tsar.

When the pleasures of killing guys started to wane, Ivan allegedly taunted the ultimate terrified prisoners. Then he traveled to the households of his patients, to gloat a few more. The story is going that after he arrived at the residence of the wealthy former treasurer, Funikov-Kartsev, he tortured the dead guy's spouse, the better to make certain he must seize all her gadgets. He then have become his interest to her daughter, whom he handed over for the pride of his son. Both have been simply fifteen years of age.

Later, the large cauldron become employed to boil his patients till the flesh fell from their bones and they screamed for the end of their suffering. No doubt, on the identical time as this end up occurring, Ivan himself became in turmoil. His crazed thoughts might be switching the various ecstasy that looking such suffering brought, a experience of justification for the rightfulness of his actions, a pious pride for performing within the manner of his private interpretation of his God's dreams, and simple satisfaction that his electricity have become being an increasing number of embedded inside the lifeblood of his petrified u . S .. Later ought to come the guilt, observed with the aid of the penance he enacted upon himself, beating his very personal frame even as prostrate earlier than a few spiritual icon or particular.

Then the self-justification that he became acting out the choice of his God may go back. And with it, all yet again the want to torture and homicide in addition harmless sufferers.

If the slaughters of Moscow lacked the scale of Novgorod, however they are despite the fact that on the maximum surrender of man's inhumanity to guy.

It is hard to count on the reasons for such barbarity. But it seems as though, to Ivan, his punishments had been justified with the aid of God — they pondered his interpretation of the bible. The problem for those he centered grow to be that this have turn out to be the Bible interpreted via way of a madman. Added to this is the truth that Ivan absolutely enjoyed inflicting pain. He had completed in order a little one on the innocent animals he flung from the excessive domestic home windows of his palace and that thrill of causing pain had continued. But it had had to come to be ever greater immoderate for him to be satisfied through manner of his repair.

The most effective break from the catalog of ache he caused fell in the end of the short length of his marriage to Anastasia.

Chapter 6: Heading For Defeat The Livonian War

It is of no surprise that an lousy lot of the tsar's time as chief of Russia turn out to be spent at warfare with one opponent or awesome. We have heard of his ongoing struggle with the Tartar armies. The first rate incredible struggle in which he engaged emerge as the Livonian conflict.

Once the Volga had been secured, Ivan sought access to the west. He believed that a safe path to the Baltic sea should help him to consistent more potent buying and promoting family members with the wealthy markets of western Europe.

Unfortunately, Livonia (it certainly is positioned in what's these days Latvia and Estonia) stood in the way. Early in the campaign, Russia made some a success incursions right proper right into a overseas land, but the Livonian's allies Lithuania and Poland came to their beneficial useful resource. Then Sweden joined in at the opponent's aspect. Seeing their traditional enemy below stress, the Tartars attacked from the Crimean, even carrying out as a long way as Moscow. They set the city on fireplace, the Kremlin being one of the few homes to live undamaged.

The Livonian warfare lasted for an remarkable twenty-four years and fine ended whilst Ivan started out to understand that defeat faced him. He sought arbitration from Pope Gregory XIII. The head of the Catholic church agreed and sent his emissary, Antonio Possevino to installation an armistice.

Ivan held on to strength in his hometown, but at a price. He become pressured to give up all his profits in Livonia, and surrender some cities inside the Gulf of Finland. For someone with the satisfaction of Ivan, this turned into humiliation in the extreme. And, of route, it come to be his folks that paid the penalty.

THE FALL OF THE OPRICHNIKI

papers exist recording the appropriate data of the oprichniki. Most likely, they have been created to beneficial beneficial resource Ivan as he fought towards Boyars who resisted his reforms.

Although they have got an notorious feature in Russian statistics of the era, the oprichiniki simplest lasted for seven years, from 1565 to 1572.

Ivan blamed them for failing to save you the assault of the Crimean Tartars on Moscow. Heads rolled, virtually, and a number of the homes, treasures and lots of the land that that that they had confiscated were back to their actual proprietors.

But but the brevity of their reign, nothing can reduce the horror this mystery military imparted on the Russian humans. Their lifestyles coincided with the maximum barbarous a part of Ivan's time as tsar. The fury, anger, and insanity that re-emerged following the death of Anastasia changed into to the fore, but he moreover possessed the properly being of frame (commonly) and emotional power to perform the worst extremes of his brutal rule.

It is of no marvel that this era matched the time of the oprichiniki's predominance.

VIDEATH

"I am a Christian and do now not devour meat in Lent."

Ivan the Terrible

Eventually, continually, the tsar's vicious temper got the better of him. In 1581 a controversy burst out among his son Ivan's wife and him, in some unspecified time inside the future of which he abused her. To be blunt, he beat her up. Violently. So violently that she miscarried the child and inheritor, she changed into sporting. Ivan did the unthinkable and stood up in opposition to his father.

DEATH OF A FAVORITE SON

Even regardless of the reality that he idolized his son greater than in reality all of us but living on the planet, Ivan the Terrible struck out along together with his employees, causing a deep wound to his son's head. The extra youthful guy collapsed. He lingered on for severa days in advance than becoming but every one-of-a-kind sufferer of his father's wickedness and uncontrollable mood. Albeit, this time an accidental one. It changed into an act from which Ivan may also want to by no means get better.

Feodor, the tsar's distinct son, have end up the heir. But he changed into prone, incompetent and childless. Ivan saw now not first-class the demise of his favored son however also of his part of the Rurik dynasty. This can also now, he feared, end up no greater than a quick-lived deviation in his u.S.A.'s facts and of the house of Rurik's prolonged reign.

He have turn out to be wracked via manner of guilt and consumed by grief. And that made, if viable, his paranoia worse. His already feeble preserve near on reality apparently collapsed altogether. He appealed to Queen Elizabeth the First of England for asylum. In a decided try and both assuage his guilt and justify his immoderate behavior, he drew up prolonged lists of those he had finished. They might be very lengthy lists virtually.

Having robbed the monasteries of their wealth only some years in advance than, now he paid them to say prayers on his behalf – something to address his guilt. He even, as his loss of lifestyles approached, ordered that he be rechristened. He decided directly to spend the previous few months of his life reborn as a monk.

DEATH OF A DICTATOR

Ivan become fifty-four years antique at the same time as he died. He turn out to be gambling chess whilst he collapsed. His opponent have grow to be one of the few men whom he depended on, his bodyguard Bogdan Belsky. It is notion that Russia's first tsar succumbed to a stroke. His orders have been that he grow to be to be buried wearing his monk's addiction in a totally remaining determined attempt to achieve God's forgiveness. He had no need to spend his eternity in the hell to which he changed into surely destined.

A LEGACY LOST

For the few short years of his marriage to Anastasia, Ivan had started the device of bringing Russia collectively and making it a splendid usa. But he spent the very last a long term of his existence tearing that legacy apart.

The Moscow he left at the back of have turn out to be destitute, damaged and in chaos. A big void crammed the hollow his despotic existence had left. Russia become a much massive u.S. Than the most effective wherein he had seized power as a boy all the ones years ago, but no matter its geographical greatness, its sources had been stretched, it modified into vulnerable to attack, and its human beings have been downtrodden and afraid. Indeed, the entire destiny of Russia lay on a knife region.

Perhaps, despite the fact that, one first-rate came from Ivan the Terrible's reign. Such changed into his manic devotion to

God that he ordered the building of a great colossus, which have become the brilliant Moscow monolith this is St Basil's cathedral. It served as a shrine to his tremendous achievements, appreciably the seize of Kazan.

Supposedly, so the tale is going, Ivan have come to be so moved with the aid of the first-rate building that he ordered its architect, Postnik Yakovlev, to be blinded actually so no extra lovable constructing must ever be created via him.

Neat as that tale might be, it is probably untrue. An exaggeration carried at the severa myths surrounding the brilliant tyrant. Yakovlev is credited with the design of numerous one of a kind spiritual and royal homes in the years to come, that is a difficult fulfillment for a blind guy to craft.

Despite the concept of religious worship in the name of this edifice, St Basil's grow to be no more than a physical expression of Ivan's egocentricity. It have end up a temple to himself, dwelling its existence within the again of the masks of being a shrine to God.

Chapter 7: A Glimpse Of The Past Clears The Way To The Future

"I am obliged to record that, on the prevailing moment; the Russian Empire is run through lunatics."

Maurice Paleologue, French ambassador

Ivan the Terrible have emerge as born at the 25th of August in 1530 in Kolmenskoye, an imperial property situated surely outdoor the historical metropolis of Kolomna. Ivan turn out to be handiest 3 even as his father died and his mom, Elena Glinskaia, turn out to be made regent. It did now not take prolonged for the electricity-hungry boyar households to begin plotting and scheming toward mother and son. Numerous tries had been made to gain more wealth, land, and energy in any manner they will. The famous model of Ivan's tale is one wherein he performs the mad, volatile, viciously cruel oligarch. He is portrayed as an anomaly while in truth, his conduct seems to be very an awful lot the norm consistent with the instances in which he lived.

It might be that resentment, coupled with superior intelligence, led Ivan down a direction of no return. His actions, looking returned, seem to stem from an anger and lust for revenge. But in the days of Ivan's reign, possibly his actions were additionally borne of worry: worry of dropping his ancient past and family proper to the seat of Tsar of All the Russias. After his father's lack of existence and the demise of his mom in 1558, whilst he became 8, Ivan and his extensively handicapped more more youthful brother had been left within the care of council individuals and Prince Ivan Telepnev Obolensky. Prince Ivan have come to be supposedly Elena's lover and political fantastic pal till his imprisonment quickly after Elena's dying.

To understand Ivan IV's desires for Russia, and actually to better apprehend Ivan IV himself, we need to delve in short into the time earlier than Ivan's tsardom. If we appearance handiest at the period in the course of Ivan's reign, we may be forgiven for wondering he initiated many thoughts of his personal and the reforms he located into area might be visible as precise and unique. In reality, Ivan emerge as following through with thoughts that have been within the pipeline due to the truth the rule of his grandfather, Ivan III, and his father in advance than him.

Ivan III have come to be Grand Prince of Muscovy in 1462 whilst he succeeded his father, Vasili II. So, we see Ivan IV emerge as in masses of methods now not simplest forging a brand new course for Russia however additionally quality a legacy that may be traced back to his remarkable-awesome grandfather, Vasili II. Vasili II took over from his father, Vasili I, on the clean age of ten, in 1425. His mother, Sophia of Lithuania, acted as regent.

Vasili II reigned from 1425-1462. His reign become dominated thru manner of civil battle as well as internal familial struggles that came at once from his uncle and cousins as all of them vied for his name. It is through this information that we discover the roots of Ivan the Terrible's so-referred to as insanity. And we should very well finish that Ivan IV turned into in no manner mad or paranoid. He behaved very much like most rulers and boyars earlier than and at some diploma in the 15th and sixteenth centuries. Betrayals and power struggles have been commonplace. Within the ruling family, and people of the boyars, there have been many instances of imprisonment, poisoning, and mutilation.

When Vasili II have grow to be Grand Prince in 1425, his feature changed into right away contested through his uncle, Yuri of Zvenigorod, who felt he had the right to rule due to a clause that changed into drafted with the aid of his and Vasili I's father, Dmitri Ivanovich Donskoy. This modified into earlier than Vasili II were born, and the clause modified into meant for an instance in which Vasili I had borne no heir.

As soon as Vasili II won the perceive at age 10, he had to combat for his rightful throne, Yuri went to the Khan of the Golden Hordes who, at the time, ruled lots of the land surrounding all the unbiased states of what would ultimately become Russia. The Khan demanded tributes from all the grand princes, and in pass again they were left to rule their sections and worship their manner. So, Yuri lower lower back with a license to rule. He took over

Muscovy and after a short incarceration, Vasili II modified into freed and given the city of Kolomna to rule. This turn out to be to expose Yuri's downfall as Vasili II plotted his revenge and in the end took his rightful place. When Yuri died in 1434, his son, Vasili II's cousin, Vasili Kosoi (additionally referred to as Vasili the Cross-eyed) took over. Dmitri Shemansky, the other cousin, right now aligned with Vasili II, and they proceeded to take down Vasili Kosoi in advance than he left the Kremlin in 1435. Then Dmitri Shemansky betrayed Vasili II, and in 1446, had him and his own family incarcerated. Four days after their seize, Dmitri had Vasili II blinded. Eventually, at the insistence of the metropolitan of the time, Dmitri released Vasili II. Vasili directly plotted his revenge and reclaimed his throne.

In 1449, Vasili II ratified Ivan III as the following grand prince, this have grow to be symbolic extra than some thing and turned into a strategic circulate to allow the humans to end up aware about the idea that Ivan III become the subsequent in line. Vasili II changed into approached through the Grand Prince of Tver, and Ivan III turned into promised in marriage to the daughter, Maria. This induced the annexing of Tver and in the end positioned an give up to the battle amongst Moscow and Tver which were ongoing on the grounds that 1300.

It grow to be at some stage in Vasili II's time that the Golden Hordes broke up into smaller khanates, Constantinople turn out to be sacked, and the Ottoman Empire rose up. We see that the commonality that runs via each generation of this a part of the Rurik dynasty is the innate desire to hold immediately to as a minimum one's call and energy, whilst on the identical time moreover trying to gain extra land, greater wealth, and more electricity. This come to be the start of the movement to centralize Russia and royal strength.

During his reign, Vasili II may not have completed all he were given proper right down to do, but he had managed to decorate Russia, and the unification the various first-rate territories had started out. During Ivan III's reign, we can see extra definitely how the course modified into laid out for Ivan IV to maintain, with lots fulfillment, to mix the impartial Russian territories, removing the wealth and land from boyar families, paving the way for eventual serfdom, and elevating his degree of authority and electricity to that of Tsar.

Ivan IV's grandfather, Ivan III, have become Grand Prince of Muscovy in 1462, extremely good twelve at the time and already married to Maria, daughter of the Grand Prince of Tver. He, too, had to go through thru bearing witness to the blatant acts of ruthless disloyalty from internal near own family ranks. He hung out hiding in a monastery to avoid being killed off thru way of enemies. He had ten years of tutelage from his father, and at some point of this time obtained enjoy in navy and diplomatic endeavors. Perhaps this is wherein the paranoia that manifested so obviously in Ivan IV commenced out. And if that is so, in all likelihood it end up not plenty a intellectual imbalance as it have become a legitimate and inbred worry of chance — threat upon their titles, livelihood, and honestly lives. It end up very real and the stakes have been high. Not satisfactory did they've got to devise and strategize to extend their territories, moreover they needed to be constantly on shield towards jealous, energy hungry family and the Aristocracy.

The right judgment in the back of wanting to amplify changed into to obliterate competition and collect an empire. When small independent states were scattered, it intended outdoor forces like that of the Ottoman Empire should with out problem invade and take over their land. The risk from unbiased states moreover supposed his very own call modified into underneath risk due to the fact the treachery and disloyalty got here from very close own family and ran via to most of the households of the boyar tradition.

Ivan III led a success campaigns closer to the Tatars inside the south and the east. He however had to pay tributes to the Khan, however so long as they have been paying their tributes, they might despite the fact that exercise their Orthodox religion and enjoy a degree of safety from the Khan, if need be. This modified into now not reciprocated, however, and whilst the Khan sought safety in Moscow at some point of his issues, he have emerge as grew to become away.

Ivan III annexed Novgorod in 1478 and delivered the pomestie device. During his reign, he tripled the Russian territory, broke loose from the dominance of the Golden Hordes, and remodeled the Moscow Kremlin. His prolonged reign end up later known as the "Gathering of the Russias." Initially, he made his grandson, Dmitri, his successor, and Vasili III and his mother had been despatched away. But in 1500, Vasili III commenced out to devise his revenge, and Ivan III ended up denouncing Dmitri, sending him and his mom away. Vasili III end up Grand Prince and stored Dmitri imprisoned till he died in 1509.

Chapter 8: Life Before The Tsardom: 1547-1560, The Early Years

"Autocracy is a superannuated form of presidency that could healthy the wishes of a Central African tribe, however now not the ones of the Russian humans, who are an increasing number of assimilating the subculture of the relaxation of the area. That is why it's miles impossible to maintain this shape of presidency except via the usage of violence."

Nicolai Tolstoy

Vasili III emerge as very aware, because of his private facts, that Ivan IV is probably centered, and the threat that he might be killed or usurped was very actual. Whether Vasili III had a premonition or whether or not he changed into best a in advance logician, he made a very clever choice and drew up a trendy will. He installation a Regional Council of seven members, a number of whom had been from the Boyar

Council. He elected Mikhail Iurevich Zacharin, who he have come to be very near, and Mikhail's nephew, M.V. Tuchov Morozov. Prince Ivan Vasilivich Shuisky of the Suzdal princely extended family and his brother, Vasily Vasilevich, who have become the most senior and authoritative member of the Boyar Council, had been elected. Perhaps maximum strategic of all come to be the election of Elena's uncle, Mikhail L'vovich Glinsky. He held no declare to the throne and can make certain the safety of the Grand Princess and Ivan. Vasili III died of a looking wound brief thereafter. He modified into buried as a monk and renamed Varlaam.

In 1554, Prince Ivan Telepnev Obolensky have become delivered to the Regional Council; it's miles rumored that he have become Elena's lover. He delivered with him his sister, Agrifena Chelydnina, who've emerge as Ivan and his brother's nanny and governess. Together with Elena, Prince Ivan got all of the manner down to remove any competition that threatened more younger Ivan's become aware of. Members of the council were each imprisoned or killed, and a few starved to loss of existence while incarcerated. These moves bred a whole lot hatred inside the course of Elena and her death in 1558 changed into in all likelihood homicide via poisoning. Soon after, Prince Shuisky took control, sending Agrifena to a convent and locking Prince Obolensky as tons as starve, actually as he and Elena had finished to others.

The period that located for Ivan and his deaf and dumb brother, Yuri, changed right into a dark one. Left with out each person who emerge as unswerving and loving in the course of them, they have been inclined on all degrees. Ivan was subjected to mental abuse with the aid of manner of using Prince Andrei Shuisky. He turn out to be constantly informed that he had a brother who changed into older than him. Ivan's father couldn't have kids with his first spouse, and so he divorced Sophia and despatched her to a convent. Legend has it that she may additionally moreover furthermore or won't have had a son, meaning she would possibly have been with infant already earlier than he banished her. And so, this boyar could probably torment Ivan IV every day, by telling him his out of place brother might cross again and take his throne.

Ivan changed into a completely religious infant, in all likelihood thru necessity truely as a terrific deal as through manner of lifestyles. He might spend as a fantastic deal as five hours a day in observance. He genuinely understood his feature and believed he changed into ordained without delay through using God. When he have become Tsar at the age of seventeen, he rose above the energy of the metropolitans, popes, and bishops. He had an absolute truth that his cause modified into to do God's will.

There is such stark evaluation a few of the Ivan that respected God and the Ivan who tortured many human beings and seemed to experience it, in line with legend, but they certainly continue to be the equal character. He modified into now not schizophrenic, however he had deep contradictions inner. There is some other mindset we do no longer entertain; possibly it's been noted earlier than and for some reason been ignored. And that is the mind-set that attempts to look Ivan as he surely became, with out judgment. If one appears on the time he lived in, we apprehend he have become part of a way of existence that displayed hardcore forms of cruelty toward traitors and enemies.

Impalings, drownings, mutilations, and starvation were all types of torture normally practiced as a shape of punishment.

So, changed into Ivan the Terrible actually so horrible? The archaic definition of "terrible" connotes a as a substitute more agreeable shape of due to this once more in Ivan's day than it does at gift. The irony is that each meanings in form him similarly. As formidable, robust, and in advance thinking as he turn out to be, he changed into moreover mainly susceptible to violent outbursts and mood tantrums. These signs, coupled with a growing experience of betrayal and suspicion in the route of the boyars and advisers he modified into surrounded through the use of way of, introduced approximately a volatile mixture of sadism, ruthlessness, and paranoia.

We have a propensity to check the alleged movements of Ivan as a boy, torturing animals and reputedly doing so with delight, as a few thing much like these days's serial killers and psychopaths. But in the large photo, he modified into surrounded by way of using adults behaving so. It changed into the way all people lived and emerge as the reality of his lifestyles. If you, as a little one, are uncovered to seeing such cruelty taken out on fellow humans, it could properly become normalized and therefore proper, and torturing an animal may occasionally appear wrong.

Ivan have become an athletic boy and cherished searching. Could it's far that his intelligence and bloodlust brought about a hobby about killing, torturing, and maiming? If he grow to be the use of animals to exercise for future acts of torture on humans, need to he be excused? It turn out to be, despite the whole thing, a few thing he is probably predicted to perform as ruler, without a doubt as his father and grandfather earlier than. Or did he act toward animals the manner he had been handled thru people?

There had been two elements to Ivan's sense of proper and wrong, it seems. The one facet should perform atrocities or as a minimum supply orders to achieve this, and the other facet would possibly famend the sin of his movements, and he is probably completely repentant and are seeking out for out council right now with God. The duality and paradox of his moves and responses will normally be puzzled and stay simplest a set of feasible theories, and this is partly why we're intrigued by way of Ivan the Terrible. His fervent religiosity have become as an awful lot an actual a part of himself as his outright ruthlessness come to be. He took possession of his role as effective chief and dominated the manner he noticed in form. During Ivan's reign, he apparently killed three,000 humans in my view. Whether this vast variety is a fact we is unverifiable, and what about the plenty that died on the fingers of his legions below his command? Who can forget about the massacre at Novgorod in 1570, in which Ivan set his navy on his non-public humans with devastating affects?

Against seemingly dire odds, Ivan survived his youngsters and in some way managed, at seventeen, to prepare his very very very own coronation. He named himself Tsar of All the Russias and maintained the characteristic of absolute monarch claimed with the useful resource of his grandfather once more in 1482. By being topped Tsar, he politically multiplied his function to that of preceding Byzantine Emperors and Tatar Khans, who have been at times every acknowledged with titles of tsar. This discover no longer best doubled his have an effect on and supremacy as chief and king but moreover tied his electricity to religion. The new identify secured his throne and additionally boosted his importance, way to the religious connotations as a "divine" leader, located in strength to enact God's will. The divine nature of the Russian monarchy modified into henceforth crystallized during Ivan's reign.

Chapter 9: Ivan The Tsar Of All Russia From 1547-1560

"Remove one freedom steady with technology and shortly you could haven't any freedom – and nobody could have located."

Karl Marx

Two weeks after Ivan IV turn out to be coronated and had obtained the Monomakh's cap, he entered into marriage with Anastasia Romanovna. He had selected her from an prepared line up of all the eligible "virgins" of the time. By all payments, their union regarded to be one in every of love and mutual respect, but we want to ask if Ivan moreover selected her because of the reality he may also moreover additionally have known her because of the family ties she had to the Zacharins, who were near his father. Whether Ivan have become truthful to her or not is controversial, however they did have a partnership and he did love her. Ivan positioned protection, and with Anastasia by way of the use of his facet, he in the end had a person he may moreover need to accept as true with. Anastasia is stated to have had a chilled effect on Ivan. This is possibly because of the fact that she supported him and he felt solid collectively along with her. They had been married for thirteen years and she or he bore him six youngsters, 3 of whom died either at transport or before accomplishing kids. Tragically, she died in 1560. Her lack of life changed into to have dire consequences for the populace underneath Ivan's rule. Her loss of life devastated him.

It is quite likely she modified into poisoned intentionally but moreover quite possible that she died of mercury poisoning because of the fact she changed into being dealt with for an contamination (in all likelihood with mercury). Mercury became a commonplace medicinal potion used all through the medieval instances. It grow to be used to treat sexually transmitted diseases along facet a group of other maladies. Little did they consider that it killed a ways greater than it healed, and the fact that signs and symptoms and signs of madness often supplied in sufferers with syphilis may additionally additionally moreover well have been from the mercury and no longer the sickness. We understand Ivan himself have become being treated periodically with the silver solution.

It have become inside the route of his years with Anastasia that Ivan professional his maximum non violent and maximum revolutionary length. Between the years 1547 and 1560, peaceful reforms and modernization were formulated and executed. It have come to be additionally all through this era that he efficiently annexed Kazan and Astrakhan. He shaped an military called streltsi devices. In 1549, he created the Zemsky Sobor, a shape of Russian parliament, on the aspect of a Council of Nobles. He showed the vicinity of the Church by using the usage of forming the Council of 100 Chapters, specifically the Stoglavi Synod. He moreover brought self-government in the northeastern regions of Russia that have been no matter the truth that very rural. In 1550, he revised the regulation code of 1497, called the Sudebnik. And in 1553, he introduced the primary printing presses thru the use of organising the Moscow Print Yard.

In 1497, Ivan III created a code of regulation based totally definitely at the genuine regulation code of the historical Kievan Rus, called Russkaja Pravda. Ivan III's code modified into called the

Sudebnik. In 1550, Ivan IV set about seeking to deliver order to Russia after almost two a few years of lawlessness following independence from the Tartars. A an entire lot-needed reform changed into called for to combat the bribery and corruption taking vicinity on administrative levels, and regulation of some type emerge as needed to maintain society from entire anarchism. He commenced out with the aid of using collecting together a flow into segment of Russian society which protected ecclesiastical and monastic authorities, members of the boyar council, consumers, and tradespeople. Not all contributors had the same authority, and an meeting become normally referred to as thru the Tsar via a letter sent out. They might be briefed as to the agenda after which gathered to talk approximately or correlate the wishes of the Tsar in phrases of law or reform.

The first Zemsky sobor, referred to as the Sobor of Conciliation, accrued in 1549, and as soon as the members had been in region, they set about revising the Sudebnik of 1497. What they got here up with have emerge as the Sudebnik of 1550. Drawing considerably from Ivan III's code, the individuals dealt conservatively and meticulously with the revisions, which incorporates new improvements. Previously, the code had prohibited judges from accepting bribes, officials from the usage of the tool for personal vendettas, clerks from filing faux facts, and jailers from selling prisoners. But those guidelines were by no means implemented, and the punishments for such acts had been by no means special. So, Ivan set about to rectify these subjects and revised his Sudebnik to encompass the suitable nature of fines and punishments that is probably meted out for the various offenses.

The men in price of formulating these revisions had to cope with a large number of offenses from the number one authorities degree, to the metropolis vice-regents (namestriki), proper all the manner right down to the rural vice-regents (volosteli). Many vice-regents had previously held army positions, and as quickly as their carrier modified into entire, they were given those dependable regency posts. They took it upon themselves to build up profits and food from citizens underneath their jurisdictions. They felt entitled, as they had received no pay while serving in administrative center. They additionally felt no loyalty to the populace underneath them as their posts usually handiest lasted a couple of years. This resulted in rampant over taxation and, basically, huge daylight robbery of the peasantry and lesser nobles in their provinces.

Ivan have been aware of court cases toward the vice-regents' behavior considering that adolescence, and with the draft of the ultra-present day Sudebnik, the authority of the vice-regents become reconfirmed and their responsibilities improved. But the massive government have become given greater control over the vice-regents in a bid to lower this exploitation.

The 1550 Sudebnik moreover made provisions for peasants that had suffered injustices on the palms of vice-regents and their marketers to convey fits in opposition to them at the crucial government degree. But whether or not or now not because of an oversight or whether intentional (in lieu of repayment for beyond issuer) the consequences in opposition to the vice-regents remained much much less extreme than those in opposition to the important authorities.

This judicial and administrative corruption modified into an inner problem that the new Sudebnik addressed, and the overall public fitness and safety troubles that had to be revised had been seen as outdoor issues.

Russia in the mean time come to be beset with famine, drought, and fires which propagated chaos and lawlessness. Gangs of criminals sprung up, concentrated on the rural villages, pillaging, raping, murdering and burning down entire hamlets. District elders below order from the maximum essential government were in price of arresting and charging the brigands. The vice-regents, however, were disinterested in following up, so revisions had been made for costs of brigandage to be brought in advance than the essential government. Thus, the 1550 Sudebnik changed into a much harsher code in principle.

It additionally dealt with faux accusations, even as the '90 seven model did not. Many infractions and crimes were punishable through using flogging or superb and "in addition punished because the sovereign shall decree." Certain articles dealt with "injured honor," once more stipulating who might be compensated and for a way an entire lot, depending on a choice of things. It additionally went beyond judicial and administrative reform and specific how the beauty device come to be to be installation. It laid forth phrases and situations regarding economic transactions and circle of relatives people between and inside the precise social agencies. But the 1550 Sudebnik made best superficial modifications to the clauses and articles concerning the mass of Russian peasantry.

There have been moreover thirteen articles concerning the business enterprise of slavery. The Sudebnik became revised now not to provide the specific commands greater freedom or benefits but as an alternative to curtail any form of interest that could advantage any given organization rather than america of america and the Tsar. Articles were installed place to save you human beings hoping to break out a few form of penance or restriction with the useful resource of entering into slavery from doing so. Provisions were made for difficult hard paintings, and some historians consider slavery turn out to be declining for the duration of this time in Russian in pick out of more modern forms of exertions.

Perhaps the vicinity left most inclined thru using the chaos within the land turned into that of land tenure, and at the same time as the Sudebnik handled the easy troubles, it became the manuscript, titled "the Tsar's Questions," that delved deeper to investigate the reality of what became going on behind Ivan's decrease lower back. Here, we see Ivan looking for to lower the Church and monasteries from gaining greater tracts of land. Slightly obtuse criminal pointers were added to try to dissuade this from happening, however in particular we see his strategies as a manner to adjust and accurately file all land tenure transactions. If negative humans lost land to the boyars who had bought it with money from monasteries, the law said that the land had to accumulate decrease lower back to the primary birthday party, and no cash was to be refunded. The reforms with the most political importance were the ones proscribing the electricity and function an effect on of the vice-regents which could possibly have been a part of Ivan's approach to restrict boyar electricity and wealth.

The Sudebnik have emerge as absolutely purported to reform judicial manage and preserve public safety, however looking greater broadly, it can encompass political and monetary hyperlinks some of the beauty systems of Muscovite society. Shortly after its final touch in 1555, activities passed off which rendered big quantities of the Sudebnik inapplicable. By 1556, Ivan's authorities was reason on shutting down the control of the vice-regencies, leaving further quantities of the Sudebnik obsolete. This circulate modified into pretty possibly a ploy to recoup land and increase the Moscow treasury coffers that have been bankrupted from all of the conquests.

It seems in all likelihood that hundreds of the Sudebnik's content material grow to be drawn up with the aid of presidency officers with out masses input from Ivan who did not care heaps for legalities. This may not be accurate, though, and in all likelihood it modified into just that Ivan changed into above those laws. They did not examine to him, and he should destroy them and exchange them as he observed in form. He did, but, understand entire well prison recommendations had to be in region to rule wherein he could not physically be. He became the free cannon in all this, his actions often in conflict alongside alongside together with his rules.

Chapter 10: All That Is Holy

"The Tsar is with the aid of nature like every guys, but in electricity he's similar to the Supreme God. And in fact as God wants to hold anybody, so the Tsar need to keep the entirety this is project to his strength from all harm, each spiritual and bodily."

St. Joseph of Volokolamsk

To surely see the depth of Ivan's delusional depravity, we need to try to understand his courting with God and the Church. We need to apprehend the place the Church had played in Ivan's life due to the reality that begin, similarly to the position the Church performed as an influential governing body of the kingdom.

Vasili III changed into the primary Russian monarch to wield so much energy. But his rule emerge as now not absolutely autocratic, and hundreds electricity and have an impact on have been notwithstanding the reality that held with the aid of way of the Church and the Boyar Council. In topics of u . S ., picks were reached by way of way of Vasili III and the Boyars. The metropolitan had the right to intercede on behalf of in reality anybody that had fallen out of favor with the Grand Prince. The gadget come to be no longer inexperienced, and even as quickly as choices have been made, the severa clerks, who also came from nobility, had the very last say. They were some distance extra prepared within the each day on foot of affairs, worked more tough, and knew greater than the boyars. This gave them a high quality effect over the boyars, and it's been advised that now and again, boyars had been dragged off and supplied earlier than the tsar with the useful resource of these clerks at the same time as boyar behavior riled them. This changed into executed to curry preference with the tsar. The concept that he turn out to be to rule on behalf of God have become given energy via severa individuals of the church that still had agendas to preserve the land and wealth of Church constant. It seems that those power plays among u . S . A . And church, and nation and king, and king and church had been persistent and slow in the development that finally brought approximately Ivan disturbing entire power in 1964.

Ivan changed into christened at the Troitsa-Sergeyrskey Monastery, which become sacred to the Holy Trinity and to St. Sergius of Radonezh. It is stated that Vasili III located Ivan atop the saint's tomb and prayed, "O, Sergius, with the aid of the use of your prayers to the Holy Trinity, you gave me my son. Protect him from all evil, visible and unseen, till he has grown in electricity. All my faith is positioned in you."

By Vasili's motion of placing Ivan on pinnacle of the tomb, the destiny Tsar have become formally dedicated to St. Sergius. Then he grow to be christened with the aid of the usage of Cassian, the barefoot monk. He turn out to be named Ivan, this is the Russian model of John, and became so named after John the Baptist. He turned into blessed at the icon of the Holy Virgin. This supposed he acquired invocations of the Holy Trinity, St. Sergius, the Holy Virgin and John the Baptist. Thus, all his life, Ivan believed he grow to be divinely blanketed.

In 1532, Ivan's father, Vasili III had a church built on the Kolmenskoye grounds to commemorate Ivan's starting. The Church of Ascension come to be designed with the useful resource of Italian developers and designers. It changed into one of the first actual tent-roof stone church buildings to had been constructed within the vintage Russia. It but stands in recent times and is at the UNESCO World Heritage Site list. By the time Ivan have end up born, the Byzantium Empire had fallen, and the Holy Church of Rome whose headquarters have been in Constantinople not had a say over the Russian Orthodox church. Moscow had succeeded in imparting itself due to the fact the "third Rome." The separation supposed that the Russian Orthodox Church changed into now not tormented by every the Renaissance or the Reformation.

It have become popular to erect a church to commemorate an event which encompass prevailing a conquest or to honor a start. So, after the sacking of Kazan, Ivan set out to fee some other church. The cease end result changed into remarkable, and St. Basil's Cathedral turn out to be created. Known as the Cathedral of Vasili the Blessed, it have become finished in 1561 and remains to these days, precise to Russian shape. It is constituted of 9 fundamental chapels. The extensive tower is a tent-roofed bell tower named the Church of Intercession of the Mother of God to commemorate the day on which Kazan end up sacked formally, the day of the Feast of the Intercession. It appears an amalgamation of haphazardly located, onion-domed towers, however the selected amount and place is rumored to be both a duplicate of Jerusalem or a image of the nine-pointed celeb. The four domes pinnacle four octagonal towers of four chapels, each specifically named. In among those are constructed four smaller chapels, every consecrating the sacking of Kazan or a war touching on that factor.

Another church that turned into constructed to commemorate his coronation and perceive of Tsar changed into the Church of St. John the Baptist at Dyakovo. The church stands by myself and other than the numerous others built close by, through way of Vasili III. Dyakovo is placed close to Kolmenskoye, Ivan's birthplace.

In 1551, at the same time as Ivan known as the Zemsky sobor, he put forward a chain of questions, directed at the clergy and pertaining hundreds in part to land tenures as become referred to in quick in Chapter three. The final outcomes end up the Stoglavi Synod of 1551, recounted moreover as the a hundred Chapters. It is well definitely worth noting that of his maximum depended on advisers, the nicely-professional, informed, and religiously fanatical priest, Sylvestri, and the similarly legitimate Alexij Adashev were critical council people and in particular influential preference makers on the time. These guys appeared to have

have an effect on over Ivan, and Sylvestri want to be identified for retaining Ivan in check for a length through instilling in him a sense of correct behavior as is befitting to an absolute monarch and servant of God. When this have an effect on over Ivan modified into out of vicinity, Ivan released into a mission to obliterate all who opposed him and, even worse, all the ones he concept were opposing him. By 1563, he perceived that every one people who went in opposition to him in even the slightest way have been really out to interrupt him.

The Stoglavi synod have become an initiative to unite the Church towards a developing heresy in addition to to adjust rituals and approve the rituals which had been in conflict with Greece. It handled church belongings and education further to ceremonial rituals and the stipulations that needed to be fulfilled with the aid of the clergy and the clergymen. The motive became to make sure that the Church maintained its function in making ready and instructing destiny monks. A powerful faction of the clergymen rejected this synod and refused to apprehend it as an authoritative textual content. The Stoglavi additionally installation the church's authority over its writers and icon painters. All the questions and answers were divided into a hundred chapters and feature come to be the easy code of canon law and a guidebook for the clergy of Moscow.

A large a part of Ivan's lifestyles have become spent making organized for and taking area pilgrimages. Once a 12 months, he would possibly make the adventure to Troitsa-Sergeyrskey Monastery, in which he were christened, to want to his icons, ask for blessings, and furbish the priests with presents, yet again soliciting for extra benefits. He might probable frequently journey to small monasteries around america, praying on behalf of his subjects, asking God for advantages, and paying his manner with devices of money, land, and probably even food. The pilgrimages have been costly affairs as Ivan traveled with a massive entourage that have become reachable to cook dinner and smooth and convey at some point of the adventure. Supplies of meals and refuge can also want to had been transported at the issue of all the people. It should were pretty an agency, as delays have to arise alongside the manner when conditions were too moist and muddy to excursion.

It became in this form of pilgrimages (after the victory over Kazan) that Ivan stopped in at the monastery in which Maxim the Greek have become living. Maxim changed into an vintage scholar who were exiled due to his heretic critiques. He had on the start been introduced over with the useful resource of Vasili III to translate historic texts. He changed into towards clergymen proudly proudly owning land and modified into a staunch ascetic. Eventually, metropolitan Macarii interceded for him, and he modified into released from the chains he had been stored in. Ivan had an awful lot respect for respected men of the material and grow to be disturbing to meet with Maxim to collect further blessings for the pilgrimage. Maxim rather rebuked him, pronouncing that his project become stupid; he may also want to reap God's need right right right here. Was it now not more important to take care of the widows and orphans left over from warfare? Did he not understand he did not need to journey so far to wish? Lastly, after Ivan modified into regardless of the reality that no longer taking his advice seriously, he ended with a curse, saying that if Ivan did now not heed his terms, his younger seven-month-old son, Dmitri, have to quickly die.

Ivan persevered on in his way. Stopping at some different monastery, he came to the abode of Vassian Topokov. Topokov have been sent away and demoted from bishop of Kolomna some years in advance for acts of cruelty and violence. Ivan requested him, "How can I rule and make the the Aristocracy obedient to me?" The solution got here, "Let no man wiser than you maintain propose over you. Be enterprise and all guys will in shape within the hole of your hand." This solution perfect Ivan, and he endured on his manner.

Soon after this, his son modified into dropped, by coincidence, proper right into a river and upon hoisting him lower again out, it modified into decided he modified into dead. Ivan end up distraught and usually chastened. For a short period, he allowed everything to run with out problems and with out excessive reprisals and cruelties. But the uneasy alliance among Ivan and his trusted advisers changed into brief lived.

Several years later, at the same time as Anastasia fell sick, it turned into Sylvestri and Adashev who've been given Ivan's blame. Jealous boyars and the equal accursed Vassian Topokov fueled those mind of Ivan, and each Sylvestri and Adashev were condemned. Sylvestri have end up locked up in a monastery and Adashev become removed from carrier in Livonia and died swiftly thereafter of a fever. Without the stern and watchful eyes of Sylvestri, Ivan's rise up knew no limits. The terror that modified into Ivan have end up approximately to be unleashed.

Chapter 11: The Wars And The Battles Lost And Won

"War does not decide who is proper — handiest who's left."

Bertrand Russell

The years preceding to the Oprichnini and Ivan's descent into insanity, while rather peaceful and powerful, were years spent strategically gaining floor and electricity. The reforms that have been hooked up took care of best a part of Ivan's large picture, and he had complete time navy preparing and education and going off to wage wars for you to claim land. The awesome warfare turn out to be one in which the army had most effective to annex the land without carrying out war. The price of these struggle-certain expeditions were very costly, and the Moscow treasury became nearly depleted thru Ivan's lengthy and ordinary campaigning.

The earliest fulfillment came in 1552 whilst Kazan have become claimed. Ivan spent most of his time praying within the path of this advertising and marketing campaign and earlier than they embarked on it. He believed certainly there may be a victory if God noticed healthful, and he did all in his strength to appease God with a pilgrimage to Troitsa-Sergeyrskey Monastery. He left with an adornment of gold and awesome treasures that he become to provide earlier than all of the icons and to the monks in price, as was the manner of lifestyles of the Orthodox faith they practiced. He supplied prayers to the icon of the Holy Trinity after which he went to desire earlier than the relics of St. Sergius. He labored his way down, imparting prayers and soliciting for blessings. He ended up at the tomb of St Peter the Metropolitan after which subsequently asked Macarii for his advantages, too. Even in the course of the siege of Kazan, Ivan spent his time presenting up prayers, and even as their final victory got here and Kazan have become theirs, Ivan knew in truth that he had received this victory way to his prayers. This changed into the campaign in which we see Ivan's non secular nature in movement.

Andrei Kurbsky were a relied on adviser and army guy that Ivan have to depend on, however even he reached a element wherein he need to not cause with Ivan and he defected to Poland, plenty to Ivan's chagrin. Of the many that suffered at the impulsive hand of Ivan, 3 men in reality did get away his instantaneous wrath and therefore prolonged their deaths. They were the priest, Sylvestri, Alexij Adashev, and Andrei Kurbsky. Sylvestri were his mother's confessor and became trusted with the resource of Ivan after the priest had helped Ivan advantage some fame with the general loads.

After a bell tower had collapsed, a terrible fireplace had destroyed Moscow, killing 2,000. The hearth have turn out to be known as the Great Fire of Moscow. All these signs and symptoms and symptoms had been referred to through the superstitious and they were beginning to name for blood, even accusing Ivan's mom-in-regulation of being a witch. Ivan changed into being blamed no longer directly and had to cover from the irritated mobs. Sylvestri stood up and proclaimed that those activities have been the end result of God's judgement, and if Ivan would definitely repent, God may need to start showing extra kindness to the humans and the united states. Shockingly, Ivan wholeheartedly repented, begging forgiveness, and the crowds had been obtained over. Sylvestri acquired Ivan's preference and all changed into well, however no longer for prolonged. In the cease, Sylvestri and Alexij have been visible to betray him whilst, upon one in each of his ailments that nearly noticed him die, he requested them to swear allegiance to his little one son if he have been to die. They refused. After he miraculously recovered, he changed into livid, and that they each left his issuer however were no longer carried out like many in advance than them. The family members of those men had been not so lucky and have been punished on those men's behalf.

Andrei's dissent surely compounded to Ivan that everyone changed into surely out to get him. This country of thoughts coupled together with his savagery delivered approximately the myth that Ivan changed into purposefully plotting and scheming to obliterate the entire boyar manner of lifestyles. It changed into the preceding twelve months that his brother, Yuri, had died similarly to Anastasia and metropolitan Macarii. Once he changed into regular and some distance away, Andrei commenced out correspondence with Ivan. This correspondence have become an vital frame of 16th century Russian literature. It survived thru the a long time and gives a first rate check out the specifics of that generation as well as into the minds of Ivan and Andrei. The style of writing at the time had a very unique layout which Andrei followed however Ivan, being Ivan, veered off from the formality of the epistles and launched into dialogues peppered with every day occurrences. This led Andrei to reply through way of way of telling Ivan to prevent babbling like a stupid lady. This form of communique demonstrates that they knew each different well, being of comparable age further to each being informed and intelligent.

After taking Kazan in 1552, a part of the Volga river turn out to be now Ivan's territory, so by the point he annexed Astrakhan in 1556, he had claimed the Volga and opened alternate routes. He furthermore freed the numerous Russian slaves, destroying the slave marketplace.

In 1558, the 24-365 days lengthy war called the Livonian War, or the First Northern War, started out out out. Initially, it became started with the cause of gaining access to the Baltic Sea's change routes. Besides Russia, the Kingdom of Sweden, the Grand Duke of Lithuania, the Polish Lithuanian Commonwealth, and the Teutonic Knights of Livonia were part of this war. Initially, Ivan did nicely. Eventually, however, the value of the struggle destroyed the Russian economic machine, whilst the antics of the oprichnina destroyed the government.

By 1579, after Ivan's peace proposals have been denied, Stefan Batory and his navy released a marketing campaign in the direction of Moscow. Stefan Batory had emerged as a dynamic chief of the united enemy the the front. In 1579, he reclaimed Polotsk. In 1580, Velikie Luki modified into taken, and in 1581, Psokov, Narva and Estonia had been received. All in all, the give up end result of the 24-yr conflict ended a good buy similar to it had commenced out, minus an extended way too many lives and at high-quality monetary fee to all involved.

Chapter 12: The Teror Of Ivan The Terrible: His Madness, Mania, And Murderous Methods

"To make certain, dictators are cunning, evil geniuses with top notch firepower at their disposal. They also are brutally green at intimidation, terrorism and mass slaughter. However, a pressure is able to dominate because of the truth the counter stress is each non-existent or willing."

George Ayitte

In 1543, Ivan ordered the execution of the boyar, Andrea Shiusky. It has been informed that he ordered his huntsmen to set the dogs on the boyar, who've been the primary instigator in attempting to persuade Ivan of the curse positioned on him with the useful resource of manner of his father's first spouse and saved alive rumors that he had an older brother, who need to cross decrease back whenever to take the throne. After this incident, the boyars began out to recognize they'll have created a monster. After his coronation, no matter the reality that he had managed to gain the name of Tsar, his electricity have become despite the fact that confined and the Boyar Duma (Council of Nobles) but held a lot sway. While that they'd historically been legislators of Kievan Rus and advisers to the Grand Dukes inside the past, with the expansion of land, alternate was needed. But this come to be not the most effective reason. In in advance instances, the Church had wielded identical, if not at instances more, strength over the throne than the actual Dukes themselves. Vasili III had started out curtailing the ones strength plays at some point of his reign, and Ivan surely persisted to fight in opposition to the ones guys and the power they constantly attempted to wield over him.

Despite an splendid majority of boyars that preferred to oust Ivan, there had been a few noted men that supported him. One of those men become metropolitan Macarii. Macarii were one of the few clerics that has stood thru metropolitan Daniel and Vasili III while he divorced Solomonia and married Elena. He additionally had the useful resource of Andrea Shuisky, and this boyar made him metropolitan over Moscow in 1542. Macarii changed into Ivan's maximum trusted adviser, frequently left in charge of the whole thing even as Ivan changed into away. He changed into instrumental at the number one Zemsky sobor and moreover gave plenty input into the Stoglavi sobor at the synod of 1551. He changed into very decided out and penned many books. He died in 1563, and his lack of lifestyles, at the facet of that of Anastasia 3 years previous, have become maximum possibly every other cause for Ivan's grief that over time become seen via way of way of historians as mental deterioration. After Macarii's demise, there has been no person that Ivan need to be given as right with or depend on to help him rule. It furthermore explains why Ivan ended up fleeing to Aleksandrova Sloboda in 1564 and traditional the Oprichnini. The small village north of Moscow carrying out being the capital of the Oprichnini from 1564-1581.

The reforms Ivan desired to place into impact meant that the nobility's land may be taken from them for the u . S ., lowering their power. But whilst he positioned those mind ahead to the Boyar Council, they rejected his regulations. This drove Ivan to a fury that led to him figuring out to percent up his whole own family and depart the Kremlin.

In 1564, he left Moscow for Aleksandrova Sloboda. From here, he penned   letters.

One changed into sent to the boyars, and the alternative to the common human beings. In the letter to the boyars, he admonished them for his or her disloyalty, treason, and corruption. In the possibility letter, he cited the boyar corruption and treason as some element he turn out to be disgusted with the aid of way of and riled the humans up towards the ruling beauty. By doing this, he won well-known assist of the lower lessons and similarly remoted himself from an already strained coexistence together together with his so-called advisers and administrators. He said that he become abdicating as Tsar and at once withdrew from all sports that required his approval, causing masses stress and worry many of the Boyar Duma and the clergy who couldn't log off on something with out the Tsar's approval. His situations, if he had been to return, had been that he may also advantage absolute electricity. This modified into his situation, and he was granted it. But the harm changed into carried out and a modern-day direction turn out to be set.

One fact that records can in no way confirm with absolute truth is that of Ivan's right country of thoughts. To what quantity were his choices stricken by natural, cold hatred within the path of any individual who dared question his techniques, hostile his proposed reforms, or admonished his conduct? Was he driven with the resource of some perverse satisfaction? Did he punish and humiliate people to boost his absolute authority? Did he recall he have turn out to be doing God's work? Did he hate doing what he did however experience that it modified into his obligation? Was it a combination of a number of these elements, or have become he driven to some extent of no go back in which he now not had the potential to accept as authentic with and refused recommendation or rebuke due to the fact he were driven over the brink with the useful resource of but each one of a kind company of individuals that he observed as disloyal because of the fact that that they had differing viewpoints on how Ivan need to cope with people. Any shape of wondering referring to his thoughts or actions, and Ivan's fury had no obstacles. Ivan had commonly validated cruelty at the same time as dispensing punishment, and lengthy earlier than the Oprichnini existed, Ivan changed into already properly versed in ordering horrendous punishments.

Ivan remained at Aleksandrova and began an extensive, immoderate vetting machine as he accrued together his private military. This navy have become to turn out to be the terror that humans partner Ivan with. The Oprichnini turned into a pressure that struck terror in the hearts of all and sundry that observed them coming.

He accrued his troops about him and that they have become an impenetrable regulation unto themselves. Ivan separated his nation into elements. He determined on land and sections at will and renamed the factors the Oprichnini and the Zemschina. The Oprichnini changed into for the Oprichniki to rule and pillage and arrest whomever they saw in form. People had been periodically added to the searching hotel and each in my view dealt with with the useful aid of Ivan or tortured beneath his command. Oftentimes, they might just experience about, inflicting mayhem and terror. They all sporting black, and it is been said that Ivan, too, dressed like this. They spent a large detail in their day amassing, fasting, and praying, and it turn out to be stated they lived like clergymen with Ivan as abbot. They addressed each different as brother. What made them appear so ruthless changed into their conviction that they had been decided on by means of God (that's what they had been taught with the aid of way of Ivan) and what they had been doing end up in truth ordained. They rode round with puppies' heads connected to their saddles and carried brooms. This turn out to be to reveal they could maul their enemies like dogs and sweep them away with out masses try. The areas demarcated as Zemschina were to be run and administrated thru the boyars.

The men had to swear their whole entire allegiance to Ivan. The oath they had to take went a few aspect like this: "I swear to be reliable to my Lord the Tsar and to his kingdom, to the more youthful Tsareviches and to the Tsaritsa, and I swear now not to be silent approximately any evils I recognize of, those who I even have heard or will pay attention about, which might be contemplated via this or that character toward the Tsar and Grand Prince, his state, the younger Tsareviches and the Tsaritsa. I moreover swear an oath that I shall no longer eat or drink or have any dealings with, or have some aspect in not unusual with, absolutely everyone from the Zemschina. On this, I kiss the Cross."

The land Ivan confiscated have become given to the Oprichniki, the preceding tenants or landowners have been solid out and needed to flee. If they have been stuck lodging nearby or receiving help from peasants alongside the manner, they might be killed or tortured. The Oprichnini loved the particular privilege of being Ivan's quality close to and trusted contrary numbers, and the men he had at his issue have been sincerely as ruthless as Ivan.

They moreover had a good buy have an impact on over Ivan and regularly their terms, whispered in his ear, caused human beings being targeted as traitors and loads of innocent, properly-which means men out of region their lives manner to the Oprichniki's determined efforts to hold their army of terror from being disbanded.

Chapter 13: Ivan's Final Years And Final Curse

"Oh Satan! Why have you ever planted one of these godless seed in the coronary coronary heart of a Christian tsar from which such fireplace swept over all of the Holy Russian land."

Andrei Kurbsky

Ivan constantly had respect for the metropolitans, and he became fortunate enough to have had the steering and facts of some well metropolitans throughout his reign. Metropolitan Philipp modified into one such man. And his goodness changed into the shortage of lifestyles of him. He was moreover the remaining upstanding metropolitan to serve in some unspecified time in the future of the rest of Ivan's reign. All folks who got here after him have been spineless, self-serving guys who did not try to prick Ivan's judgment of proper and wrong in any way.

Before Philipp modified into appointed, Metropolitan Afanasi held the location. It grow to be in the course of considered certainly one of Ivan's trips away that Metropolitan Afanasi left his placed up, pleading infection. He retired to the Chudov Monastery located inside the Kremlin partitions. It is idea his contamination have emerge as know-how too much of Ivan's sins. Ivan changed Afanasi with every other exemplary guy, Herman Polev. Polev have become the Archbishop of Kazan, a person of tremendous physical stature and massive holiness. He wasted no time in telling Ivan that he end up on the wrong route and it might be clever to disband the Oprichnini for the sake of Russia in addition to for the welfare of Ivan's soul. Ivan changed into inspired with the holy man's speech and stated his communication decrease lower back to one in each of his crucial henchmen, Alexei Basmanov. It did no longer take an entire lot convincing on Alexai's thing to sway Ivan's desire to get rid of Herman. Fortunately, he had not been formally inducted however, and Herman became loose to move returned to being Archbishop of Kazan, changing tartars to the Christian religion.

Ivan then summoned Philipp Kolychev who changed into the abbot of the Solovetsky Monastery within the some distance north. Philipp attempted to refuse the publish, but Ivan ought to no longer pay attention of it. Philipp then stated he might also need to obtain the submit excellent if the Oprichnini had been abolished. Ivan ought to no longer agree. It changed into a stalemate. The boyars glad Philip to take the put up as they held him in excessive esteem, his recognition for being a God serving, righteous guy gave the boyars a glimmer of desire. Perhaps Philipp could be capable of quell the Tsar's penchant for torture and repair a semblance of peace to Ivan's fragile, paranoid thoughts. So, he popular the positioned up and agreed no longer to intrude with the Oprichnini or with Ivan's affairs.

The first speech Philipp gave as metropolitan lessen at once to the chase, and he raised the troubles maximum important on his mind. Ivan listened and stated no longer a few factor, biding his time. Eventually, almost years later, Ivan and his men entered the church wherein Philipp became giving mass and demanded a blessing. Philipp refused to bless him, mentioning that his get dressed and his ongoing behavior did no longer warrant a blessing. His words have been recorded with the useful resource of the clergymen that were present and remembered via foreigners, Taube and Kruse. Metropolitan Philipp replied Ivan like this:

Even in heathen kingdoms, regulation and justice prevail, and there may be compassion for the people—but now not right right here! Here, the lives and possessions of the humans are unprotected, anywhere there's pillage, anywhere there may be murder, and all this is perpetrated in the call of the Tsar! You take a seat down excessive in your throne, however there may be a God who judges us all. How will you stand in advance than His judgment seat, stained with the blood of the innocent and deafened via their screams under torture! Even the stones below your feet cry out for vengeance! I communicate, O Tsar, because of the reality I am a shepherd of souls and I fear simplest the first-class and handiest God!

Even after this curse upon Ivan, the Tsar did no longer act without delay. He started looking for some component scandalous that he must use towards the metropolitan. But they stored springing up empty handed, even after interrogating his courtroom docket or even going decrease decrease lower back to Solovetsky Monastery in which Philipp had lived for thirty years. Ivan feared the wrath of the complete Church if he had been to kill Philipp, so he continued to look for proof. Eventually, Philipp changed into framed by the Oprichnini, and he emerge as arrested. An abbot by using the call of Paissey consented to signing fictitious claims in opposition to Philipp. Ivan had him carried off in chains to be imprisoned and left to starve.

Miracles began to stand up. First, the chains fell off him, and while men came to check on him in his mobile, he became popularity in his cellular, praying. They then set a 1/2 of-starved endure on him within the cellular. When they once more, the undergo changed into snoozing within the nook and Philipp prayed. They decapitated someone near him and taken him the severed head; he kissed it and blessed it. News of the miracles travelled and crowds accumulated. Ivan, fearing a revolt, had him moved to Otroch Monastery. Metropolitan Philipp modified into tortured, degraded, starved and so very wrongly accused and in the long run killed, but up until his final lack of existence breath he in no way stopped caution Ivan to trade his methods and saved appealing to him to try this, no longer for Philipp or for Russia, however to keep his very very own soul. Sadly, via this time, Ivan have become manner beyond any element of pass returned.

It changed into in 1580, nice 4 years in advance than Ivan come to be to die, that Russia conquered Siber (Siberia). Yermak Timofeyevich have become the Cossack chief that have been commissioned with the resource of manner of the Stroganov own family to protect their lands, given to them with the useful aid of Ivan to increase and create income. Yermak managed to triumph over the Siberian lands for Russia. He sent word to Ivan and requested reinforcements which Ivan thankfully sent. Ivan duly have come to be Tsar of all Russia and Siberia.

For all his debauchery, his many marriages, and his murderous strategies, Ivan became a found out guy. He loved to observe, he preferred art work and shape. He modified into musical and composed himself. He become additionally poetic and loved to engage thru letter writing. These letters have been to lend masses perception into the existence and times of Ivan. While some college students argue those were seventeenth century forgeries, others acquire as proper with them to be genuine. In 1581, after beating his daughter in-regulation for dressing immodestly, his son faced him. Apparently, Ivan struck him and he died; Ivan grow to be devastated. He had killed the heir to his throne. Some assets say this is truely extra myth that has sprung up in the course of the story of Ivan.

He died in 1584 at the same time as playing chess, likely of a coronary coronary heart attack. In 1963, his body modified into exhumed and theories emerged suggesting he may additionally additionally had been strangled or poisoned. So an awful lot intrigue and thriller has been infused into the story of Ivan the Terrible. We can also in no way understand the overall fact, but. He struck worry into the hearts of absolutely all of us, buddy or foe.

Chapter 14: Who Was Ivan The Terrible?

Ivan IV Vasilyevich, referred to as Ivan the Terrible in English, modified into the Grand Prince of Moscow from 1533 to 1547 and the first actual Moscow ruler to announce himself Tsar of Russia from 1547 to 1584.

Ivan turned into the first ruler of Moscow after the city's flexibility. After the loss of life of his dad, Vasili III, the Rurikid ruler of the Grand Duchy of Moscow, he was declared outstanding prince whilst he modified into 3 years of age. The "Chosen Council," a hard and fast of reformers, rallied at some stage in the younger Ivan in the year 1547, saying him tsar (emperor) of All Rus' and advanced the Tsardom of Russia, with Moscow because the number one state. Ivan's rule modified into marked by means of manner of Russia's change from a center a while kingdom to an empire beneath the control of the tsar, but at a massive price to the human beings and the country's lengthy-lasting economic system.

Let's speak about his existence, his legacy, his evil deeds, and the way subjects befell in records.

The khanates of Kazan and Astrakhan have been dominated within the direction of his boyhood. After combining his energy, Ivan disregarded the "Chosen Council's" specialists and released the Livonian War, which damaged Russia and brought approximately the dearth of Livonia and Ingria, but moreover generic him to establish greater autocratic energy over Russia's nobility, which he purged strongly with the Oprichnina. The Massacre of Novgorod and the Tatar burning of Moscow happened within the latter years of Ivan's reign.

Ivan's precise person is portrayed in diverse techniques in modern assets. He modified into considered amazing and religious, but liable to fear, rage, and episodic bouts of intellectual instability, which intensified as he elderly.

He killed his oldest little one and successor, Ivan Ivanovich, in a in shape of rage, and he may also need to have moreover induced the miscarriage of the latter's pregnant little one. That left his more youthful infant, the politically inefficient Feodor Ivanovich, to accumulate the throne, a man whose control and following childless demise right away brought to the Rurikid dynasty's demise and the start of the Time of Troubles.

Chapter 15: His Youth

Ivan have come to be Vasili III's first teen with Elena Glinskaya, his 2d companion. Vasili's mother end up a Byzantine Palaiologos relative and a Greek princess. She changed into the daughter of Thomas Palaiologos, the younger brother of Constantine XI Palaiologos (r. 1449-- 1453), the final Byzantine Emperor. Elena's mom modified into a Serbian princess, and her dad's circle of relatives, the Glinski line (nobles from the Grand Duchy of Lithuania), said family tree from Orthodox Hungarian nobles and also the Mongol king Mamai (1335-- 1380). Ivan's dad exceeded away whilst he modified into three years of age from an infection and infection on his leg that became blood poisoning. At his dad's advice, Ivan modified into stated Grand Prince of Moscow. Elena Glinskaya acted as regent within the starting, however she exceeded away within the 365 days 1538 at the same time as Ivan become super 8 years of age, and masses of take delivery of as proper with she was poisoned. The regency became then handed back and forth among many competing boyar households defending manage. According to Ivan's private letters, the super boyars from the Shuisky and Belsky households regularly unnoticed and outraged him and his greater more youthful brother Yuri. Ivan recalled in a letter to Prince Kurbski, "They raised my brother Iurii, of holy reminiscence, and me as drifters and destitute youngsters. What have I lengthy past via without a doubt because of a scarcity of garments and meals?" The ancient analyst Edward Keenan has puzzled that story, questioning the authenticity of the document in which the prices lie.

Ivan changed into topped with Monomakh's Cap on the Cathedral of the

Dormition on January sixteenth, 1547, while he changed into 16 years of age. He have grow to be the number one person to be declared "Tsar of All Russias," partially in duplicate of his grandpa, Ivan the Third the Great, who stated the emerge as aware of of Grand Prince of All Russias. Till then, Muscovy's rulers were called Grand Princes, but in his correspondence, Ivan the Third the Great defined himself as "tsar." Ivan wed his first bride-to-be, Anastasia Romanovna, a Romanov family member and the number one Russian tsaritsa, 2 weeks after his crowning.

Ivan become crowned tsar to speak a message to the area and Russia that he changed into now the kingdom's sole outright ruler, and his will could not be puzzled. "The new discover represented the presumption of powers just like and similar to those had via the use of the preceding Byzantine Emperor and the Tatar Khan, each of whom were defined as Tsar in Russian assets. Ivan's function rose because of the political effect ". The new title not handiest ensured Ivan's rule, however additionally gave him a cutting-edge degree of electricity that have become inextricably connected to religion. As "church works unique Old Testimony rulers as 'Tsars,' and Christ because the Heavenly Tsar," he end up now a "extremely good" leader despatched out to perform God's motive. The freshly given grow to be aware of have become consequently given down the generations, and "being a success Muscovite rulers ... Benefited from the first-rate nature of the Russian queen's strength, which combined at some point of Ivan's reign."

Chapter 16: His Domestic Policies And Rule

Regardless of the catastrophes delivered on with the beneficial aid of the Great Fire of 1547, Ivan's rule changed into marked thru tranquil reforms and modernization. Ivan changed the regulation code, developing the Sudebnik of 1550, developed a standing military (the streltsy), advanced the Zemsky Sobor (the number one Russian parliament of feudal estates) and the council of the nobles (referred to as the Chosen Council), and tested the position of the Church with the Council of the Hundred Chapters (Stoglavy Synod), which mixed the wearing activities and clerical suggestions for the whole He superior close by self-authorities to backwoods taken with the aid of america of the united states peasants, specifically in northeastern Russia.

In the twelve months 1553, Ivan ordered the shape of the Moscow Print Garden, and Russia got its first printing press. Some Russian religious guides had been posted inside the 1550s and 1560s. Standard scribes have been dissatisfied with the brand new innovation, and the Print Garden was burned down in an arson attack. Ivan Fedorov and Pyotr Mstislavets, the primary Russian printers, had been compelled to barren region Moscow for the Grand Duchy of Lithuania. Regardless of this, e-book printing rebooted inside the 12 months 1568, with Andronik Timofeevich Nevezha and his child Ivan in rate of the Print Garden.

To rejoice the capture of Kazan, Ivan had St. Basil's Cathedral constructed in Moscow. According to custom, he have become so eager at the building that he blinded the designer, Postnik Yakovlev, so he may additionally need to never ever create whatever as fascinating again. Though, within the early 1560s, Postnik Yakovlev created a few churches for Ivan, and moreover the partitions of the Kazan Kremlin and the chapel over St. Basil's tomb, which become located as much as St. Basil's Cathedral some years after Ivan's demise. While that name has been related to a couple of favor fashion fashion designer, it is idea that the number one clothier is the precise equal person.

The first pointers restricting the motion of peasants, which could in the long run bring about serfdom, have been enacted on the time of the rule of thumb of thumb of future Tsar Boris Godunov inside the 12 months 1597.

Oprichnina

The 1560s delivered issues to Russia, prompting Ivan to move his suggestions substantially. Dry spell, starvation, failed fights in competition to the Polish-- Lithuanian Commonwealth, Tatar intrusions, and a sea-trading barrier enforced thru the Swedes, Poles, and the Hanseatic League damaged Russia. Anastasia Romanovna, his first marriage partner, surpassed away inside the yr 1560, likely due to poisoning. Ivan emerge as significantly impacted through his private catastrophe, that is regarded to have affected his person, if now not his psychological fitness. In the intervening time, Prince Andrei Kurbsky, one in every of Ivan's therapists, defected to the Lithuanians, took command of Lithuanian soldiers, and broken the Russian vicinity of Velikiye Luki. Ivan superior a paranoid suspicion of the Aristocracy because of the collection of treasons.

On December third, 1564, Ivan left Moscow for Aleksandrova Sloboda, in which he sent out 2 letters revealing his abdication due to the top class and clergy's declared robbery and treason. In Ivan's lack, the boyar courtroom turned into helpless to rule and feared the Muscovite human beings' rage. A boyar emissary changed into dispatched to Aleksandrova Sloboda to bring about Ivan to get higher the throne.

Ivan consented to transport lower back on the situation that he take shipping of whole energy. He asked for the functionality to determined accountable, carry out, and take the property of traitors with out disturbance from the boyar council or the church. Ivan ordered the oprichnina to be built.

That turn out to be a one-of-a-kind terrain inner Russia's borders, specifically inside the antique Novgorod Republic's terrain within the north. Ivan changed into the quality ruler of the area. The zemshchina (' land'), the kingdom's 2nd branch, became controlled with the aid of the Boyar Council. Ivan moreover have been given the help of the Oprichniki, an man or woman bodyguard. It emerge as initially appointed high quality the year 1000.

Malyuta Skuratov supervised of the oprichniki. Heinrich von Staden, a German traveler, changed into one famous oprichnik. Under the oprichnina, the oprichniki had social and economic benefits. Ivan, no longer genetics or local ties, have become accountable for their loyalty and rank.

The initial wave of persecutions centered Russia's good-looking clans, especially the effective Suzdal households. On suspicious claims of conspiracy, Ivan killed, banished, or with the aid of way of pressure tonsured well-known contributors of the boyar clans. The Metropolitan Philip and the effective warrior Alexander Gorbaty-Shuisky had been some of those finished.

Ivan broadened the oprichnina to consist of 8 middle districts inside the three hundred and sixty 5 days 1566. Only 570 nobles out of 12,000 were determined on oprichniki, at the identical time because the relaxation have been exiled.

The oprichniki have been given large estates underneath the cutting-edge political form, however in assessment to former belongings proprietors, they had been now not held liable for their sports sports. "Practically all the peasants had were taken, and that they have been driven to pay 'in three hundred and sixty 5 days as an lousy lot as [they] used to pay within the yr 10," consistent with the guys. As a end result of the tyranny, there had been extra examples of peasants escaping, which decreased favored manufacturing. The charge of grain has extended appreciably.

The Oprichnina's state of affairs changed into intensified with the resource of the 1570 plague, which killed ten thousand people in Novgorod and six hundred to one thousand people each day in Moscow. Ivan ended up being concerned that aristocrats of the upscale town of Novgorod have been making plans to flaw and place the metropolis itself under the manipulate of the Grand Duchy of Lithuania on the time of the lousy situations of the contamination, hunger, and the non-prevent Livonian War.

Petr Volynets, a Novgorod close by, informed the tsar about the supposed conspiracy, which modern-day records specialists say is wrong. Ivan ordered the Oprichniki to get into the city in the yr 1570. Novgorod and the encircling cities have been ruined and pillaged with the aid of the oprichniki, and the city in no way ever recuperated its earlier price.

The variety of casualties differs dramatically relying upon the supply. According to the First Pskov Chronicle, 60,000 humans have been killed.

The killing lasted 5 weeks, in step with the Third Novgorod Chronicle. Men, ladies, and youngsters were associated with sleighs and tossed into the freezing waters of the Volkhov River on the time of the Novgorod massacre, which Ivan ordered primarily based absolutely upon unverified treason allegations. He then tortured and slaughtered endless its house owners in a pogrom. The archbishop become furthermore assassinated. Practically each day, 5-hundred to six hundred people have been killed or drowned, despite the fact that the principle dying toll only stated 1,500 big human beings (the Aristocracy) and about the perfect same huge type of tinier human beings.